Advance Praise for
Act Early Against Autism

"If I suspected an autism spectrum disorder in my child, this would be a book I'd reach for."

—T. Berry Brazelton, MD, Professor Emeritus of Pediatrics,
Harvard Medical School, Children's Hospital Boston

"Early intervention is the best weapon we have against autism. This intelligent and compassionate book from Jayne Lytel will help parents become informed and effective advocates for their children."

—Bob Wright, cofounder of Autism Speaks

"This book will help parents with a newly diagnosed autistic child to cope with their grief. It also provides good practical advice to help parents work with schools and professionals who provide therapy."

—Temple Grandin, PhD, author of *Thinking in Pictures*

"Lytel's book reminds parents and professionals that the brain's ability to change and adapt to the environment is lifelong and that hope is not only a reasonable thing to have, it is critical to achieve the best quality of life and most successful outcome for every child affected by autism, at every age. Even today many professionals are still telling parents that autism is a lifelong disorder with no hope for treatment or recovery. With our current understanding of the brain and its lifelong plasticity nothing could be farther from scientifically sound advice. Practical, useful, readable, and a moving story all at the same time, Lytel's book should not be missed by any parent of a child with autism."

—Portia Iversen, cofounder of the Cure Autism Now Foundation,
author of *Strange Son*

"A vivid and astounding story of love, loss, and recovery, with an added kicker: hard-won wisdom and solid credible advice."

—Matthew E. Melmed, JD, Executive Director of ZERO TO THREE:
National Center for Infants, Toddlers, and Families

continued . . .

"Finally, a book that doesn't just dryly recite the facts about autism. In this insightful and practical guide, Jayne Lytel captures in moving detail the vital connection between acting early and positive outcomes for children diagnosed with an autism spectrum disorder."
—Peter F. Gerhardt, EdD, president and chair of Scientific Council,
Organization for Autism Research

"Jayne Lytel's book not only addresses the truth behind autism, but embraces it with kindness and understanding for its many faces in which autism presents itself in each child. Jayne Lytel is a mom after my own heart. Both brave and humble, she trusts her intuition, surrenders to God's will, and accepts her child for who he truly is—a gift. This is the book I can only dream of writing myself, but can rest happy and assured that someone else had the courage and determination to write. Brilliant. Powerful. Honest."
—Veronica Bird Mahaffey, founder of Ahead with Autism,
sponsored by the Veronica Bird Charitable Foundation, Inc.

"This book is a must-read for parents and professionals alike. As Jayne's story unfolds, parents will immediately relate to her journey and the events that characterized it, while professionals will gain valuable insights into the emotional roller coaster and incredible challenges children and families face once a diagnosis is given. As a professional, I have rarely come across a book whose author so honestly shared feelings about having a child with a significant disability. Jayne does so with eloquent grace." —Esther Y. Marsh, LMSW

Act Early Against Autism

Give Your Child
a Fighting Chance
from the Start ▶ ▶ ▶

Jayne Lytel

A Perigee Book

A PERIGEE BOOK
Published by the Penguin Group
Penguin Group (USA) Inc.
375 Hudson Street, New York, New York 10014, USA
Penguin Group (Canada), 90 Eglinton Avenue East, Suite 700, Toronto, Ontario M4P 2Y3, Canada
(a division of Pearson Penguin Canada Inc.)
Penguin Books Ltd., 80 Strand, London WC2R 0RL, England
Penguin Group Ireland, 25 St. Stephen's Green, Dublin 2, Ireland (a division of Penguin Books Ltd.)
Penguin Group (Australia), 250 Camberwell Road, Camberwell, Victoria 3124, Australia
(a division of Pearson Australia Group Pty. Ltd.)
Penguin Books India Pvt. Ltd., 11 Community Centre, Panchsheel Park, New Delhi—110 017, India
Penguin Group (NZ), 67 Apollo Drive, Rosedale, North Shore 0632, New Zealand
(a division of Pearson New Zealand Ltd.)
Penguin Books (South Africa) (Pty.) Ltd., 24 Sturdee Avenue, Rosebank, Johannesburg 2196,
South Africa

Penguin Books Ltd., Registered Offices: 80 Strand, London WC2R 0RL, England

While the author has made every effort to provide accurate telephone numbers and Internet addresses at
the time of publication, neither the publisher nor the author assumes any responsibility for errors, or for
changes that occur after publication. Further, the publisher does not have any control over and does not
assume any responsibility for author or third-party websites or their content.

First edition: March 2008

Library of Congress Cataloging-in-Publication Data

Lytel, Jayne.
    Act early against autism : give your child a fighting chance from the start / Jayne Lytel. — 1st ed.
      p. cm.
    Includes bibliographical references and index.
    ISBN 978-0-399-53394-5
    1. Autism in children.   2. Parents of autistic children.   I. Title.
    RJ506.A9L98 2008
    618.92'85882—dc22   2007040453

PRINTED IN THE UNITED STATES OF AMERICA

10 9 8 7 6 5 4 3 2 1

PUBLISHER'S NOTE: Neither the publisher nor the author is engaged in rendering professional
advice or services to the individual reader. The ideas, procedures, and suggestions contained in this
book are not intended as a substitute for consulting with your physician. All matters regarding your
health require medical supervision. Neither the author nor the publisher shall be liable or responsible
for any loss or damage allegedly arising from any information or suggestion in this book.

Most Perigee books are available at special quantity discounts for bulk purchases for sales promotions,
premiums, fund-raising, or educational use. Special books, or book excerpts, can also be created to fit
specific needs. For details, write: Special Markets, Penguin Group (USA) Inc., 375 Hudson Street,
New York, New York 10014.

To Leo, Lucas, and David
with love

ACKNOWLEDGMENTS

Like the countless number of hours my son, Leo, spent in therapy, there are countless people to thank. First, I wish to thank my husband, David, for helping to keep our family together through these difficult years and believing in me. I am deeply grateful to author Barbara Esstman for mentoring me through the process of writing a book and pulling the story out of me when I didn't think I could remember any more. This book also would not have been possible without Joëlle Delbourgo, my agent, and Sally Stewart of SA Stewart Communications, who introduced me to her. I owe special thanks to my editor at Perigee, Marian Lizzi, who helped frame the message of my book in ways that will make it stronger and more enduring. Dennis Kneale, a dear friend and tech and media editor of *CNBC*, also deserves a huge thank-you for making special contacts for me.

More thank-yous go to the many caring and giving experts who vetted important facts in this book to make it richer. They include:

- Jeremy Buzzell, program specialist, U.S. Department of Education

- Sophia Colamarino, PhD, vice president of research, Autism Speaks

- Matthew D. Cohen, JD, cofounder of the Chicago law firm of Monahan & Cohen and LDOnLine commentator

- Kelly Dorfman, LS, LND

- Claire Lerner, LCSW, director, ZERO TO THREE Parenting Resources

- Rebecca Landa, PhD, director, Center for Autism and Related Disorders, Kennedy Krieger Institute

- Esther Marsh, LMSW, independent contract service provider

- Alicia S. Perry, PhD, private practice (Daphne, Alabama) and adjunct faculty, University of Massachusetts at Lowell

- Rebecca Parlakian, senior writer, ZERO TO THREE

- Serena Wieder, PhD, cocreater, Floortime

- Peter W. D. Wright, JD, cofounder, Wrightslaw.com

- Fred R. Volkmar, MD, director, Yale Child Study Center

I would also like to thank my faithful readers, Barbara Miller, Gail Roache, and Tom Salyers—all colleagues at ZERO TO THREE—and freelance writer Barbara Benham, who guided me with encouragement and enthusiasm. And although I list her last, she is tops in my address book—Andrea Booher. Andrea embodies the meaning of true friendship, and I thank her for capturing Leo with her professional photographic eye.

I can't change the direction of the wind, but I can adjust my sails to always reach my destination.

—JAMES DEAN

TO THE READER

The information in this book is not intended nor recommended as a substitute for diagnosing and treating your child or for legal advice. Always seek the advice of a qualified health care and/or legal professional for a diagnosis and treatment, and for understanding your options for educating your child. With few exceptions, many of the names in this book were changed.

CONTENTS

▶ ▶ ▶ Foreword

It is now over sixty years since Leo Kanner (1943) first reported on the syndrome he described as "autistic disturbance of affective contact." Although children with autism had probably been seen (but not recognized) before Kanner's work, it was his genius to recognize the commonalities of what, in some ways, seemed a diverse group of individuals. In particular he recognized that the lack of social engagement (autism) was one of the hallmarks of the condition. He also was the first to identify many other features typical of children with autism—the troubles with change, unusual motor movements, areas of unusual abilities, and atypical language development. Unfortunately some aspects of his initial description also served to mislead early investigators, for instance, in his sample, many of the parents were remarkably well educated and successful. This observation led, in part, in the 1950s to a tendency to think that parents might be involved in causing autism. There was also much confusion about autism as a diagnosis, with many researchers assuming that it represented some form of schizophrenia. As a result of all these issues, progress in understanding autism was limited, as were the few attempts at therapy.

By the 1970s things began to change for the better. As children with autism were followed over time, it became clear that their problems were not like those of children with schizophrenia. Indeed as children became older, the observation of high rates of epilepsy suggested major brain involvement and the first studies of twins with autism similarly suggested a strong genetic contribution. By 1980 autism was officially recognized and included in the landmark third edition of the *Diagnostic and Statistical Manual* of the American Psychiatric Association (APA, 1980). This recognition, in turn, led to more and better research as investigators could agree on what autism is. This led to a gradual, but continuing, increase in research. For example, between the years 1943 and 1989, about 2,900 scientific papers were published in relation to autism; between 1989 and 2004, this number mushroomed to 3,700. Reviews of recent research (such as Volkmar, Lord, et al., 2004) are a testament to the remarkable productivity of the field with advances made in essentially every area—from studies of the gene, to brain, to behavior, to intervention.

Early studies of outcome had suggested a relatively grim prognosis for children with autism (Howlin, 2005), but these studies were conducted at a time when what little treatment there was had not been guided by much empirical research and before the 1975 passage of Public Law 94-142 (Education of All Handicapped Children Act), which meant that for the first time children with autism had, along with other children with disabilities, the right to a free and appropriate public education. The interest in early intervention and autism led to the development of a range of treatment models around the United States with a large increase in the quality and quantity of research.

The National Research Council's (2001) report recently reviewed this large, and expanding, literature. It has noted commonalities as well as differences in treatments that have been shown to be effective for at least some children. Probably the most hopeful part of this report is its emphasis on treatment as presenting a major opportunity for significant improvement for many (although sadly not all) children with autism and related conditions.

This book is a tribute to the many advances that have been made as well as to the work that needs to be done. Jayne's story is a moving one that has important lessons for all parents. At the same time she rightly emphasizes the differences as well as the similarities of children with autism and the importance of taking the individual diagnosis into account in providing a quality therapeutic program. Unfortunately all too often we struggle with making the child fit into the available program rather than designing the program around the child. Also unfortunately there is, at least in my experience, tremendous variability across the country in ways that children with autism are provided services. Despite the considerable progress we have made in research, it also remains the case that, as a society, we have been much less adept at translating research findings into practice in school and home settings. At the same time it is clear that progress has been made.

When I came to Yale in 1980 to work with the late Donald Cohen, people would not know what the word "autistic" meant; often they heard the word as "artistic" and thought I was interested in doing art therapy! Now, thanks to the efforts of groups like Autism Speaks, information on autism appears regularly on television and other media. The dramatic increase in awareness has also paralleled a similarly dramatic recognition of the public health problem autism represents. A growing body of research is dramatically increasing our potential for making a diagnosis either of autism or risk for autism in the first year of life. There is good reason to believe that earlier diagnosis and intervention will lead to even better outcomes. As is illustrated by Leo's story, much can be accomplished although progress can, at times, seem to parents to be grindingly slow and laborious.

This volume will be of interest to professionals and parents alike. For professionals it offers a view of the process "from the inside"—that is, from the parent's point of view. From the parent's side, Jayne Lytel has managed to provide an informed, informative, and balanced volume designed to make parents aware of the many potential resources available to them. As she repeatedly emphasizes, it is important for parents to use this book to think carefully about their own child and his or her needs.

Fred R. Volkmar, M.D.
DIRECTOR AND IRVING B. HARRIS PROFESSOR
YALE UNIVERSITY CHILD STUDY CENTER

▶▶▶ Introduction

Trust yourself.

Listen to yourself.

Convince yourself.

There are fundamentally different ways you as a parent approach this new challenge that confronts you from the way your trusted medical professionals do. Their way is about certainty, giving you a diagnosis that has the force of their authority behind it.

You, on the other hand, will most likely want uncertainty to prevail, meaning you want above all to maintain the hope that you're up against something curable, or at least addressable, even if that runs counter to the grim assessment delivered by earnest but unsmiling men and women in white coats. You won't want to adjust to your child's limitations; you want to return to the vision you had before all this—of his or her successful, independent future life—if that is possible.

This book is about how to recover from the blow of the diagnosis, implement an intensive early intervention plan, and find your voice as an advocate for your child. With all the professionals you will consult, the fundamental therapeutic direction you take for your child is up to *you*. You are the supervisor, the case manager, the underwriter, the decision maker.

You need a basic understanding of the current knowledge about autism and what treatment alternatives are backed by the best scientific evidence, to empower you to make informed decisions with the help of the doctors and therapists.

Step up and act early, in the face of uncertainty, and you can dramatically increase your child's chances of returning to a healthier course of development, with residual issues that seem minor compared to where you began.

How do I know? I am a fifty-two-year-old mother of two little boys, now eight and ten years old. This story traces the arc of my journey—the four worst years of my life—when my younger son, Leo, began to show unexplainable behavior after his first birthday and subsequently was diagnosed with autism, a vexing neurodevelopmental disorder.

I will share how I intervened successfully to give my son back his life and me back mine, which was also derailed by his diagnosis. In my quest to recover him, I became broke, almost destitute, let down by the system that was supposed to protect me.

But in the end, I rescued Leo from autism, and once again I am in the spotlight, this time as a crusader for early intervention. It's never too early—or too late—to start an early intervention program if the red flags of autism begin to appear.

The essential challenge of Early Intervention is not *intervention*, which is action; it is the *early* part. How do you know it is early if you don't even know what sort of a problem you're addressing or if you have one at all? To me, it means two closely related things. The first is a parent's trust in his or her early intuition that something is wrong. As the understanding and awareness of autism grows among both parents and pediatricians, you are less and less likely to be told to wait and see and come back in six months, although that may, in fact, happen. If that is the case, you have to teach yourself how to ask the right questions and then find the courage to continue your query and your search for the right people to help you.

More commonly, early intervention means taking immediate action after you have received an authoritative diagnosis. In this endeavor you can expect to have a lot of support from doctors and caregivers, most all of whom will be urging you on to buy as much therapeutic intervention as you can afford. One diagnostician said to me, "We are taught to save for our children's college education, but Leo needs to spend that savings right now."

By that time, of course, your son or daughter (or niece, nephew, grandson, granddaughter, or other close relative) is already in contact with professionals that can help him or her. You, however, were there from the very start. You were the one who smelled the smoke and sounded the alarm. Act early, get an early diagnosis, and get your child into early treatment. Early, by and large, is a result of your early understanding.

The research is quite definitive that intervening early produces more progress than if intervention is started years later. But the brain—a gray and gooey three-pound mass that Galen, a physician to the Roman gladiators, was the first to recognize as the locus of emotion and intelligence—is endowed with breathtaking plasticity to adapt and change in response to its environment long into adulthood. If your child is facing autism or its related disorders, its power to adapt is the reason you and your family should not give up hope.

An early, intensive, and consistent intervention program that blends therapies anchored in science offers the best chance for you to help your child surmount, if not overcome, his or her challenges. I will tell you how I sorted through a bewildering array of treatments and chose one treatment over another and how I fought to have them paid for.

That is one of many things that you will learn, I hope, by reading this book.

My son started therapy when he was twenty-five months old, relatively young. If Leo were my first child, I may have taken longer to realize he needed help, but I can't say for sure. My intuition spoke to me, and after some denial I finally listened.

On a deeper level, my story is a reflection on relationships as the core of the human essence—how we form them and how we cannot live without them. My son's disinterest in forming relationships with people is what struck terror and panic in my soul. An inability to relate to others is the core deficit of autism spectrum disorders. I knew I could not go through the rest of my life unless I did everything I could to restore his ability—but more precisely his *desire*—to relate to people. It was up to me once again to bring him into the world.

People tell me my son's recovery was miraculous, but it was no miracle. I fought hard to get him the services he needed and persevered with the same determination as an Olympic athlete. While not all children will meet the same degree of success, any degree of success is success. I want you to feel good about yourself that you did everything you could to help your child. I know that is what you want or you wouldn't have picked up this book.

The point is, get started now and develop strategies to fit the lifestyle, culture, and financial resources of your family. You, and you alone, are your child's advocate, not the school district that is required by law to provide a "free and appropriate education" for your child, not the educational advocate or lawyer you hire, not your therapists, psychologists, and other specialists, as good as they are. You.

I did not follow any special diets, discover any quick fixes, and I do not blame the vaccine-preservative thimerosal for my son's diagnosis. I respect the great many families who believe that this mercury-based preservative in the vaccine against measles, mumps, and rubella (MMR) is responsible for triggering autism in their child, and I commend their efforts to keep this toxic heavy metal out of vaccines, especially for children, no matter how minuscule the amount. But I did not notice any difference in Leo's behavior or regression in skills after he received the MMR vaccine at thirteen months. What I saw was a pattern of behavior that led to a plateau in my son's development and that put him further and further behind his peers.

Practical Advice

In addition to my story, the "Practical Advice" sections in each chapter direct you to action-oriented advice that focuses on essential information. These sections cut through the clutter of information and offer guideposts to understanding more about autism spectrum disorders, federal special education law, early intervention, and treatment options. The intent is to tell you what this information means rather than dryly recite the facts.

The "Practical Advice" sections also include boxes labeled "FAST FACT" to emphasize a point, and "Inform Yourself," which takes advantage of a technology that has revolutionized the way we communicate—the Internet. I don't know how I would have learned what I did if it were not for the power of the search engines. "Inform Yourself" targets online resources and decodes the language of professionals to enrich your understanding of the many complicated topics you will come across.

Specifically, the "Practical Advice" sections will help you:

▸ Recognize the earliest signs of an autism spectrum disorder.

▸ Avoid a premature diagnostic conclusion.

▸ Implement a comprehensive early intervention program.

▶ Gain confidence to select appropriate autism treatments and educational programs.

▶ Understand the science and fiction of treatments.

▶ Design a Floortime and multisensory room in your house.

▶ Hire and train student therapists for home-based programs.

▶ Know when you're in for a rough ride with your school district as you navigate federal special education law.

▶ Deal with the cruelty of others who make inappropriate and hurtful comments about your child's behavior.

▶ Help siblings understand why their brother or sister is different.

▶ Cope with the emotional trauma, exhaustion, and financial stress as you seek to balance the needs of work, family, and marriage.

Use this book to empower yourself and to empower your child to succeed, because if you believe in your child, your child will believe in you. And don't look back. Your odyssey will be long. Cry when you must. We all do. It is a painful experience, and nothing in life can prepare you for it.

Of all the advice I offer, I want you to gain the confidence necessary to move forward with treatment if you believe something is wrong.

ONE

▶ ▶ ▶ # Leo's Story:
The Power of Acting Early

The tape was abandoned in a drawer in the attic. When I found it four years after my son Leo's first therapy sessions, my mind surged with emotions. I put it in a cassette deck, braced myself, and listened to my voice. It began:

> *Both reason and intuition tell me something is not as it should be with Leo. Just over two years old, he is an active little boy who virtually does not talk. He makes sounds, says words occasionally, and often talks to himself in a quiet voice.*
>
> *Our pediatrician says wait and see, but his assurance does not calm my churning conjecture about what might be wrong. Is he deaf? Mentally retarded? Developmentally disabled? Brain damaged? A sensory issue? Autism? Is it some hereditary aliment that has been lurking for generations?*
>
> *Is it my fault? Did I ignore him as a baby? Should I have had a natural childbirth? Was I in labor too long? Should I*

have had a C-section? Did I inhale something toxic when painting the living room?

My first action was to consult doctors and specialists to get their assurance that he would probably grow out of it, which they gave me. But my inner voice screamed so loud it drowned out my denial that something was wrong and that I had to find it and fix it. The most important thing I learned is to summon your courage and act, even before you have a name for what you're up against. Taking that first step as early as you humanly can gives your child the greatest chance of finding a secure place in the world.

Two weeks after I recorded those words for a radio show on September 4, 2001, a developmental pediatrician evaluated Leo and declared him autistic. His written report said:

Neurological examination revealed a self-directed, language-delayed boy who had pacing behavior. Imaginative play was infrequently seen. While Leo was able to name a picture, clap and play 'So Big,' these interactions were circumscribed, inconsistent, and infrequent. . . . The results for Leo using the CARS [Childhood Autism Rating Scale] were consistent with a diagnosis of autism.

The doctor delivered this diagnosis to us following the examination, driving both my husband and me to tears. I confess that I did not know what the diagnosis meant and my lack of understanding no doubt contributed to my terror. My research into autism up to that point had been superficial because it was too terrifying to contemplate. Seven years have now gone by and the word "autism" has not lost its shock value for me, but at that moment it meant that my son had a problem with his brain that was making him behave strangely and that he would have this condition all his life.

Anxiety washed over me, and I wondered what the doctor was telling me. Was he saying that Leo wouldn't grow up to live a normal life? That he'd be dependent upon me forever? That he'd talk to himself and have no close friends? Would he go to school or get married or get worse? Would he become violent or dangerous?

I was an older mom, forty-four at the time Leo, formally named Leonidas after a Greek Spartan king and not the candy store, was born on June 23, 1999. My only frame of reference in the area of child development was my firstborn, Lucas, who was two years older than Leo. Lucas was a handsome boy with a Gerber baby face, eyes the color of moss with tiny flecks of brown and gold, and a build that would surely make him a finalist in a sturdiest baby contest. Since birth, Lucas had a certain baby happiness about him—smiles, joy, silliness, giggles. As a toddler, he'd race around the house, then glance back to see if he had my attention before inviting me to chase him again. He was gregarious and social and gave great concentration and laserlike eye contact to the video camera as it followed him. When my mother-in-law visited, Lucas ran over and greeted her by looking up and saying hello with his eyes.

At the time all that was too normal to notice. It was only as Leo grew up not doing those things that I began to feel discomfort. Leo was a hard child to raise. He was more nimble and agile than Lucas but required constant attention. He was always crying in the grocery store or slipping off my lap at restaurants to get away. Rather than run around the house to be chased, he seemed to run to get away. He'd head out the back door, down the stairs, and around to the front of the house. If I took him back onto the porch, he'd keep repeating this path over and over again. Reading helped calm him, but I couldn't for the life of me get Leo to sniff the flowers in *Pat the Bunny* the way Lucas had when he'd been Leo's age.

When Leo was eighteen months old, I raised my concerns with my pediatrician and his nursery school teacher, but they said nothing was wrong.

With the exception of that gut feeling about Leo, this was probably the time of my life when I was most secure—emotionally, physically, financially, and every other way. While pregnant with Leo, I had begun a column about online etiquette for a local paper. When it was picked up for national syndication, I had a very part time, very high profile, very easy work-from-home job.

I had launched the first publication covering the Internet in 1993 and for my prescience appeared on television and was interviewed by scores of publications. In the early days of the Internet as a mass phenomenon, I was profiled as a "legend of the Internet," listed in *Email Addresses of the Rich and Famous*, and dispatched by the U.S. government to talk about the Internet overseas. I partied at the Aspen manse of Sun Microsystems' cofounder Bill Joy and drank with the wizards who linked the first four nodes of the Internet together in 1969. I loved my life.

My husband, David, was also an Internet professional. We met when he worked on Internet issues in the White House Office of Science and Technology Policy. We got married three years later, celebrating our nuptials with a business trip/honeymoon to Japan, giving presentations on electronic commerce for the U.S. Information Agency. Lucas arrived in 1997 and the next year we relocated to Syracuse, where David had a number of Internet-related ventures and clients. He worked at home most of that time. Money was easy (he sold a domain name for more than the cost of our 5,000-square-foot house), we had all our meals together, and we had plenty of time to play.

Against this perfect background Leo's peculiarities became more pronounced and our suspicions strengthened. I admit that I couldn't bear the stigma of having a "retard," which was the word my mom used for the "special needs" students at the school my brother and I attended in Lorain, Ohio. I couldn't help but notice her stiff posture and the heightened inflection in her voice when she saw them, signaling to me to stay far away as if they had the plague. But Mom was sensitive enough to their handicap that she would not let me point. Her views soaked in and became part of my inheritance from her.

David coped with Leo's issues more easily probably because he was so much more ferocious about taking on life. He loved the challenge of intellectual achievement, as his wall of diplomas attested. He'd survived emotional disasters like the suicide of his father when he was eight and then his brother a few years later. As a teenager, he'd recovered from a critical head injury when trying to stop a burglary. He even handled taking care of his mother as she deteriorated from Lou Gehrig's disease and post-polio syndrome, finally dying after two long years of struggle. Leo was six months old.

Other than us, David's sister was the first to notice Leo's unresponsiveness, even to his name. We had his hearing checked, but the results were normal. As Leo neared his second birthday, a neighbor referred me to the county health department, which administered early intervention services for the city of Syracuse under a publicly funded federal program. The woman I spoke with said Leo needed to see a team of therapists—a speech-language pathologist, an occupational therapist, and a special educator. They came over to my house in mid-July 2001, and stayed for a couple of hours.

When I received their report, it said:

Eye contact was fleeting. . . . Leo has significant difficulty processing sensory information. . . . Leo was in constant motion throughout the evaluation, flitting from one activity to the next except when playing with his train toys. . . . Leo is a child who prefers to play on his own. . . . He does not respond to sound.

The report labeled him as a "preschooler with a disability" and hit me with another term—"sensory integration." Baffled by this term, I entered it into online search engines and found a path of links that culminated in the devastating diagnosis of autism. No, this could not be true. I searched some more. What I found was a link to the diagnostic criteria for autism in the *Diagnostic and Statistical Manual of Mental Disorders*, known as the *DSM-IV*, the official manual for diagnosing mental health disorders.

The criteria described three impairments from the realms of social interaction, communication, and behavior. A diagnosis of autism depends on a constellation of symptoms from a myriad of criteria under each impairment. I conceded that Leo met the first two criteria involving poor social and communication skills, but I could not talk myself into conceding the third impairment that described an inflexible character; odd body movements, habits, and interests; and irrational responses to everyday sensations, such as loud noises or touch.

Minor changes in Leo's environment did distress him, as when he'd cry inconsolably at the grocery store. I'd stick a string bean in his mouth, hoping that he'd suck on it, or give him chocolate and M&M's. Generally, this worked long enough to give me time to race up and down a few aisles and fling groceries in the cart. The third criterion also described odd body movements. Leo never clapped or rocked, but I wondered if his habitual pacing qualified. I rationalized Leo's pacing as a way for him to organize himself under stress, and this gave me a way to believe that Leo failed to meet a diagnosis of autism.

Although we didn't have a diagnosis, Leo started early intervention two weeks later, at the age of twenty-five months. It consisted of three hours of speech therapy and another three hours with an occupational therapist (OT). The OT worked on his ability to touch things he didn't like. She also sang to him while he swung in a therapeutic swing. The swinging motion, she said, stimulated his body in ways that teased out language and interactions.

The department also recommended that we place Leo at a school that allowed children with disabilities to learn in the same classroom alongside their nondisabled peers. The thought of sending Leo to a special education school, even though it included typical kids, was difficult for me to accept because it was my first step into the special education community, one I did not wish to belong to.

The unsettling results of the health department's report also prompted me to call back my pediatrician to make a referral to a specialist for a diagnosis. The specialist, a developmental pediatrician, confirmed our suspicions, leading David to ask, "How autistic is he? Is it mild, severe?"

"Oh, we can't tell you that," the doctor said, as if he were expecting this question. "There's no way of knowing."

"What can we expect?"

"I can't give you a prognosis. There is no cure for autism. It's a lifelong brain disorder. But we've seen many children do very well with therapy."

As David and I left his office, I thought, *How could this be happening to me? My son looks so normal.* I ran my hand down Leo's arm, lightly freckled by the sun, and looked into his eyes. I loved Leo's eyes, so blue and translucent like pool water filtered by light.

"You can get a second opinion, but after that, you're just shopping for a diagnosis," his assistant, a nurse, said.

So what could we do? Was there any way to cure this horrible and mysterious brain disorder?

We struggled to adjust to the diagnosis. Any debate over what I should've done before Leo's birth was a moot point. Autism isn't a disorder that can be tested in utero, and even if there were a test, I would have never thought to ask for it. Still, the stress and anxiety weighed upon me, and I turned to shopping and alcohol to cope. The one glass of wine at dinner became two, then three, which helped me to sleep after days when Leo threw a gigantic tantrum or closeted himself off from me. I went shopping since it soothed me and got me out of the house. Invariably I came home with some new toy that would surely, this time, attract Leo's attention.

I also trolled the Internet to shop for treatments—probiotic supplements, horseback riding therapy, special diets, the Son-Rise Program, a lot of weird stuff. The hours I spent online exhausted and confused me but at least gave me the feeling that I was working on the problem.

As we were grieving over our awful news, the rest of the country suddenly had a sorrow of its own. One week later, terrorists attacked the Pentagon and destroyed the Twin Towers, pulling the entire world into a state of shock, grief, and anger. The disaster gave us camouflage, since we were no longer the only shoppers at Wegmans pushing a cart down the aisle in obvious emotional distress.

We enrolled Leo in the special education program, and the director of the Jewish Community Center's nursery school program allowed Leo to stay in the center's afternoon program. His special education teacher introduced me to Floortime, a therapy that encouraged engaging play to improve communication, thinking, and relationship skills. I didn't know what it was or that Floortime was part of a comprehensive model of intervention, called the DIR (Developmental, Individual-Difference, Relationship-Based) approach, but I later learned that Floortime played to Leo's strengths in language and play skills—attributes that my untrained eye could not see during those early days—and that's probably why his teacher recommended it.

She taught me that babies and toddlers pass through six developmental milestones along their path to childhood. Children with autism fail to master these milestones, and Floortime fills in the gaps. Because Lucas had developed typically, I didn't know that infants climbed these six steps, described as self-regulation and interest in the world; human relations and intimacy; two-way communication; complex communication; emotional ideas; and emotional thinking.

As I practiced Floortime, I explored applied behavior analysis (ABA), a structured intervention that is the antithesis of Floortime, yet the only widely accepted treatment of autism. A form of ABA breaks down language and other skills into their individual components and teaches each one individually using a reward system. It sounded like training a dog to sit: A pet owner provides a dog a stimulus (in this case, a command) and rewards the dog with, for example, a bone (the reinforcer) each time the dog complies. But I couldn't bring myself to learn ABA when the people I trusted, Leo's therapists, told me to stick with Floortime.

As I struggled to learn and understand these approaches, I sought a second opinion. The neighbor who had referred me to the health department told me to call Yale University's Child Study Center. Her cousin was going through the same thing with her son, and she said Yale was the best diagnostic center in the country.

I quickly learned that doctors are eager to see the youngest patients. I thought Leo had a good chance of acceptance because he had just turned two. Since many children aren't diagnosed until three or later, doctors appreciate an opportunity to more fully understand the social and emotional impairments in very young children.

Leo's diagnosis also triggered another meeting with my local early intervention office. The office called the meeting, held within days after his diagnosis, to increase his services, "services" being the word that collectively described the various therapies Leo was receiving under federal special education law, which I did not fully grasp or feel inclined to delve into then.

Unrelated to Leo's diagnosis, the Internet boom had gone bust, and David and I acknowledged that staying in Syracuse wasn't helping us financially. Although it was detrimental to the Internet political business he was now operating, he really loved our majestic house and didn't want to leave it. But we were approaching another Syracuse winter when the cost of operating three heating systems peaked at over $1,000 a month. Given Leo's intervention then under way, we made a radical decision to move back to Washington, in order to give David's business a better chance to thrive where the business of politics was headquartered. When we broke the news to Leo's therapists, they told us that they knew families who moved back from DC because services in New York were so good. Leo's therapists said the burden for finding a quality "inclusion" program, such as Jowonio, which mixed children with special needs with nondisabled kids, would likely fall on me. They said I might have to fight for it, since in DC, the number of special education complaints and hearings was the highest in the nation. If they were right, then Syracuse would be our bed of roses, and Washington would become our crown of thorns.

I called old friends to find other parents like me and made lots of calls to potential schools in the Washington metropolitan area, as if I had a quota to fill. The magic words I waited to hear were "Floortime" and "inclusion." I learned that neighboring Montgomery County, Maryland, had better special ed programs than the District. But I'd spend more in legal fees, around $40,000, if I didn't like them and had to fight for a private program. In the District, I could get away with spending under $10,000 in legal fees. I hadn't thought about moving purposely to an area that *did not* have quality public services so I could get higher quality private services paid for with public funds, as I had in Syracuse.

With that in mind, we searched for a home near a Metro stop in Bethesda, Maryland, which borders the District. Living close to the Metro was important because I anticipated needing to hire students to help with Leo's therapy. If they didn't have a car, the Metro would make it easier to get to my house. But since Bethesda offered few good choices in our price range, we crossed into the District, eventually buying a Metro-accessible house close to American University, a potential source of student therapists. The house was near a public elementary school, which Lucas would attend for kindergarten, and a highly regarded inclusion preschool for Leo right across the street.

To stay strong and motivated, I kept a diary that held the entries to Leo's emerging but significantly delayed speech. Each day, I recorded each little measure of progress. No store-bought baby books were right for this as these were not memories to capture but the empirical observation of his progress, to be presented to the evaluation team at Yale. He became my little science experiment.

A month after we bought the house, Leo completed four months of therapy, and it was now time to drive to New Haven. Upon reaching the Poconos—the halfway point—all I could think about were newlyweds, champagne glass bathtubs, and red velvet drapes in a time when life was easier and I could relax. My mind veered back and forth between indulging in the fantasy of a trashy novel and my reality of being a middle-aged woman on a life-altering course. Then, in the silence, out of nowhere, I heard his voice: "I love you."

"Leo!" I cried. I looked over my shoulder at Leo in his car seat, which engulfed his slight body, and the sun lit up his hair like golden down. My emotions collided. He had said, "I love you," spontaneously. I made a mental note to write it in my diary after we arrived. But I never did. In fact, I never wrote in my diary again.

After two days of testing, David and I met with Dr. Fred Volkmar, a world-renowned autism expert, and the other examiners to discuss the results of the evaluation. Everyone in the room leaned toward him as he started to speak. He prefaced the diagnosis with a few words, but I only remembered him saying "autism spectrum" and that Leo failed to meet all of the criteria for the disorder. He offered a new diagnosis—pervasive developmental disorder–not otherwise specified (PDD–NOS)—and the one I had "wanted." While still on the spectrum, PDD–NOS is often less severe and allowed me and Leo to escape from the devastating word "autism."

Leo had what the experts call "splinter" skills. Dr. Volkmar said Leo's gross and fine motor skills were relatively strong, compared to other children his age. And that seemed to be the key phrase—compared to other children his age. I thought about his peers anytime I had to size up Leo to measure his progress. He spoke less than fifteen words, and I didn't know how many words he understood.

A normal twenty-five-month-old toddler says up to 300 words and understands up to 900 words. Leo was thirty months old.

That softened the blow for the bad news. Leo's poor play skills, unusual sensory interests, odd behaviors, limited range of emotional expressions, poor eye contact, and lack of joint attention stood in the way of his ability to form relationships. Joint attention develops about nine months of age and involves a baby spontaneously moving his eyes back and forth, between a person, an object, and then back to the person, for no other apparent purpose than to share joy.

I clung to the positive comments like the survivor of a shipwreck looking for hope of rescue. As someone who grew up in a small town in the Midwest and attended a laid-back college in Florida, the name "Yale" had great resonance to me. The word and the place said science and authority.

Dr. Volkmar recommended year-round therapy of at least twenty-five hours per week, including ABA. I learned that applied behavior analysis could be done in a way that was less structured than sitting at a table and giving instructions. Yale's report ran for thirty-one singled-spaced pages. The report from the doctor in Syracuse, by comparison, stated his treatment recommendations in less than a hundred words.

The Yale examiners advised against medication to control Leo's temper because of his young age. It would be better, they said, to model appropriate language when Leo got upset, such as saying "no big deal" if he couldn't find his rainbow socks.

When we got home, I explored special education services in DC. I feared a gap in services once we moved, despite assurances I received from the DC early intervention office. Yale emphasized that Leo had two to three years, while his brain was still taking shape, to benefit from an intensive intervention program. After that, he could still make progress but not as much. I also was worried that if his treatment couldn't continue without interruption, he might regress.

Scouting for New Services

As Leo turned two and a half, we moved to DC, and our battles with the District of Columbia over services for Leo began soon afterward. The early intervention office gave me names of therapists to contact but none had openings, and the District never recommended a program.

Enrolling Leo in the Treatment and Learning Center (TLC) program in Gaithersburg, Maryland, which cost $400 a week, was the best alternative. The TLC program offered essential therapeutic services in a two-hour program that ran three times a week. During that time, Leo got occupational and speech therapy and Floortime. But I also started writing checks like they were Post-it Notes. To ramp up to the recommended twenty-five hours of therapy per week, I had to pay out of pocket for extra speech and occupational therapy, another $400 a week. I got a partial reimbursement in a mediation hearing, but I shouldn't have had to fight two battles—one to get services and the other to get them paid for. I vowed that when it was all over, if it ever was to be, I'd advocate for the rights of disabled children less fortunate than Leo. I would make a case to show the value of meaningful early intervention and the escalating costs that occur when a child's educational needs are not met. I would show the collateral damage to these children if early intervention wasn't taken seriously.

The money we got back from DC early intervention, however, did not pay for his home-based therapy, which cost another $250 a week. I followed through with Yale's recommendation to get one started and sought this more naturalistic approach to applied behavior analysis. I found a top-notch psychologist to train me and bought big books with lofty titles to learn more about it. I read tediously written articles on the principles of behavior analysis, while other mothers, I imagined, read *Parents* magazine. I also pounced on an opportunity to meet with Dr. Serena Wieder, a cocreator of Floortime. I knew families jetted in from all over the world to see her. Luckily, I just had to drive across town and putter up her narrow driveway.

Under the direction of two psychologists, I became the general therapeutic contractor who hired and managed a crew of students to administer a home-based therapy program. I soon formed my own opinions about what Leo needed and pursued interventions like a "ferocious mama lion," as Dr. Wieder once called me. I was also Leo's cook, driver, security blanket, bodyguard, valet, and waitress, among other roles, all of which he received with love and indulgence.

My reward was seeing Leo continue to make great strides in therapy. But then he would do something that rattled my nerves. Three months after we moved, Leo began to place his hand in front of his face every time he said a word, as if he were about to blow a kiss. I'd scan the room to see if anyone else noticed, freaking out about what this meant, what other odd behavior might surface, and whether I should bring it to a professional's attention.

With our expenses exceeding our income, we began drawing on our savings and living on credit. There was certainly a time in the future when this solution would no longer work, but we didn't know when that day of reckoning would come. To be honest, I disregarded how much money I was spending on Leo's therapy ($1,000 a week) because knowing was more frightening than not knowing. My attitude was that the life of my child was at stake, and we'd just have to find the money. If there was an opportunity to help him achieve independence through intensive early intervention, he deserved it. We would find the money because we had no choice.

We retained a special education lawyer and an educational advocate to help us navigate the system. Things got more complicated when our lawyer said to transition Leo out of early intervention and into the public school system. We needed to begin that process since he'd be turning three in June, which was when early intervention ended and the DC public school system took over. I found all this very confusing—two different entities to handle my son's services, depending on his age, a different set of people and rules to follow. Moreover, there were acronyms to learn and legal definitions to process.

I registered Leo as a "nonattending" student at Janney Elementary School, our neighborhood public school, which would trigger a meeting between us and school officials to write a new intervention plan. With that legal maneuver completed, I also applied him to St. Columba's Nursery School for the school year beginning in the fall 2002 as my backup if the school system failed to come up with a program. I knew, from talking to the director, that St. Columba's primarily enrolled children whose families lived in the neighborhood and belonged to the church. Though the church was Episcopalian, I figured they'd make room for a lapsed Catholic.

Two weeks after notifying Janney, a succession of calls and meetings between us and school system officials began. Imagine an atonal, weirdly paced symphony. First, the calls were fast and furious. Then, as David and I prepared for meetings, they slowed. The third movement resembled the more dancelike rhythm of a minuet as we maneuvered into position. The final movement ended with a rondo, a fast flurry of calls and meetings that pitted the interests of the school district against Leo's rights under the law.

In the end, we couldn't agree on the amount of services and where Leo would go to school. The District wanted to cut back on everything, even eliminate the occupational therapy that with Floortime had been the mainstay of his therapy in Syracuse. After another meeting in May, the District moved to place him in a special ed program at Lafayette Elementary School. David and I disagreed with the recommendation and refused to sign his intervention plan because the program did not include children without disabilities. Leo's intervention plan drawn up in Syracuse stipulated an inclusion program, since evidence continues to grow that students learn better and develop more social skills in classrooms with typical children.

We quickly realized that the school district was not on our side. In Syracuse, everyone worked as a team with one goal: to help Leo learn and develop as normally as possible. I didn't believe that the DC school system officials were inherently bad people; they had their orders from the school system's central office to cut costs. But I still found it difficult to accept their allegiance to the system rather than to the kids.

A bright spot of news arrived before summer 2002. St. Columba's accepted Leo, but we had to pay for a one-to-one aide. "I'll find one," I told the director. David and I cheered amid the ka-ching of the escalating cost of his intervention plan. Leo's admittance, however, didn't absolve us from observing the Lafayette program. To oppose Lafayette and request public funding for St. Columba's, we had to observe Lafayette, as did our educational advocate, who'd testify as our expert witness during a due-process hearing, a legal proceeding for contesting a school placement.

A few miles from our home, Lafayette maintained open classrooms (no walls between the rooms), despite the demise of the practice in the late 1970s. The special education students, however, had their own room, which was long and narrow like a mobile home. It had no windows, no sink, no bathroom, and only one exit for emergencies. There was so little floor space that teaching materials had to be placed off the ground on shelves that wrapped around the room.

Ms. Jones was the special education teacher. When we entered the room, she was attempting—with the help of two aides—to educate eight children with an enormous range of special needs. There were twin girls, born about fourteen weeks early, who were now three and still babbling and in diapers; a three-year-old boy with mental retardation for whom this was his third placement; another boy diagnosed with an autism spectrum disorder; and the rest of the children, the oldest being five, who had significant language and other developmental delays. Ms. Jones referred to the younger children as "the babies." When an aide was absent, a female security guard stepped in.

By contrast, a group of ten children around Leo's age, five of whom had special needs, attended Jowonio. The rest were typically developing, and the children with disabilities were somewhere on the autism spectrum, except for one child who had Down syndrome. Two aides were assigned to help the lead teacher, but sometimes there were as many as five adults in the room, usually special education majors from nearby Syracuse University.

The teaching methods at Lafayette differed considerably. To calm a little girl's tantrum, Ms. Jones turned on the TV, playing *Teletubbies*, a program aimed at infants and toddlers. She also used *Teletubbies* to stimulate the children's language and imitation skills. If a Teletubby jumped, Ms. Jones told me she said, "Jump," to show the children what the word meant. There is no research showing that the program helps preverbal children learn how to talk. In fact, the show has no proven educational value.

There were no TVs in the classrooms at Jowonio. To learn language, teachers paired sign language with words and described the children's actions in the presence of the less verbal children to help them understand the meaning of words.

Shocked, David and I returned to the car in silence. We could appreciate the burdens placed on Ms. Jones and empathized with her; I found it difficult to manage one child with special needs. But beyond toilet training, there did not seem to be any education going on at all. It wasn't even very good babysitting.

Later that evening, David and I marveled at the difference between how we were treated in Syracuse versus how we were treated in DC. The District of Columbia Public School system was a broken, chaotic, shameful bureaucratic machine in the style of the old Soviet Union. We also joked that at a banquet of DC school system officials the waiters would say, "Your choices are chicken,

fish, or beef. But since we're out of chicken, fish, or beef, we're prepared to offer you our evaluation of your protein needs."

But this was no laughing matter. On July 29, 2002, we filed for
due process, a legal proceeding.

By Labor Day, we were significantly weighed down by the
financial burden in addition to our psychological burden. Caring for
Leo and focusing on his needs had consumed us for slightly more
than a year, altering the pattern of our daily lives. "Fixing" Leo had
become our life, not a part of it. As David and I contemplated the
months ahead, we realized we needed to take a break if we were to
continue at the same intensive pace. If we didn't take care of ourselves, how could we take care of both our boys? Happily, my aunt
and uncle offered the use of their condo on Jacksonville Beach for an
end-of-the-summer retreat. During our stay, we stepped back from
the therapy and recouped. There was a small swimming pool, steps
away from the ocean. After a good long session at the beach one day,
Leo took a running jump and leaped into the water.

David and I gasped, but Leo bobbed to the surface, took a
breath, located David ahead of him, and then swam underwater to
David, grabbed on to him, and looked around.

"Leo, that was fantastic," we both exclaimed. "You can swim!
Good boy."

We celebrated Leo's wonderful self-made accomplishment of
swimming. Granted, it had nothing to do with either language
or social interaction, but it was a glimpse at Leo's strengths and
brought our thinking around to what he could do rather than
what he could not.

At Yale that fall, Leo's scores improved, sometimes remarkably,
on all fronts. His language in particular showed tremendous gains.
But the positive scores dipped significantly on tests that measured
his ability to use language for social purposes, and he rarely made
direct eye contact. As the evaluation progressed, the testing offered
a window into Leo's long-term deficits. He couldn't tell the difference

between flower and dog shapes or make a one-inch cut across a strip of paper. He was still struggling with basic skills. While he had made great progress, he retained a diagnosis of PDD–NOS.

At the end of the evaluation, the experts still recommended twenty to thirty hours a week of intensive therapy. They said we could back off from behavior modification since he had achieved most of the goals such a program can address. They recommended that we increase opportunities for Leo to interact with typical kids and said his overall social development could benefit from Floortime. Other recommendations included teaching Leo to nod and shake his head to indicate yes and no and to respond to greetings, integrating a hand wave while saying "Hi."

After we returned from Yale, I began to implement their recommendations.

The Battle over Schools

Throughout the spring and summer, I was engaged nonstop in some type of legal thrust and parry with the District of Columbia school system over Leo's placements for the summer and the next academic year. We had won at due process the first year, when they sought to place him at Lafayette. We won back the cost of his tuition at St. Columba's, all of his related services, and our legal fees, totaling $20,000, but the checks always came in dribs and drabs.

When spring 2003 arrived, we cycled through the same process, but this time the school system recommended the same elementary school as Lucas's and a summer school program at yet another public school. We stood a good chance of keeping him out of Lucas's school since he wasn't toilet trained; the teachers rolled their eyes when I asked them if they would change the diaper of a four-year-old. They did not seem to have experience with very young children with special needs, and the personal aides employed by the school district we observed seemed unqualified, inattentive, and irre-sponsible. I saw an aide, assigned to supervise a four-year-old girl with Down syndrome, play basketball while the girl wandered around the swing set alone. I pictured somebody snatching her, and it frightened me to think that girl could be my son, with no one but other children looking out for him.

When I observed the summer school program, I had heard an aide mocking a girl with cerebral palsy for beating on a file cabinet with a stick. He joked that she'd grow up to be a drummer.

We formally rejected both placements in a letter, to which we received a response restating the school district's position that Leo should attend public schools. As they had previously, the letters made up the paper trail that led to the final face-to-face confronta-tion both sides knew was looming.

Recovering Leo so that he'd talk, play with other children, and attend a regular kindergarten on his own obsessed me. I poured as much therapy into Leo as he could tolerate, but I knew when to back off. He'd either hide under the covers or curl up in a ball on the floor and pull his shirt over his head. He also cried, and as much as this is against the advice of the experts, I gave in to his wishes to stay home because I just wanted peace and quiet, know-ing that I'd have to suffer the financial consequences of not giving his therapist the required twenty-four-hour cancellation notice.

During our wrangling with the school district that spring, I cob-bled together a summer program with mornings at Basic Concepts, a speech-language camp, and afternoons at a regular summer camp run by the JCC, which accepted children with special needs and assigned them a personal aide. The program had a waiting list by the time I applied for the special needs component of the program, but the camp director said Leo could attend as a regular camper and I could pay for my own aide. I agreed, but when I spelled out the terms—Leo had to attend Basic Concepts in the mornings because it ended at noon—the director refused to let Leo into the program because she wanted him to spend his mornings at the JCC. We appealed to the executive director, who overruled her. It was a small victory and came when I needed one.

And if there had been a moment of pause, I might have felt some accomplishment, but there wasn't one. I saw nothing but a rapidly closing window of opportunity to correct Leo's course of development if he was to live an independent life, which by my math meant we had only one year left of intensive therapy. In September 2003, when Lucas headed off to first grade, he never complained that he'd be in an after-care program that lasted until 6 p.m. when we both should be home playing. Lucas had taken to soccer but Leo would run in all directions, showing no interest in the rules of the game or playing with us. When Lucas asked me why Leo didn't play with him, I struggled for the right words, getting stumped on the "why." How could I find the words to explain this complicated brain disorder to a six-year-old? I settled on offering Lucas words of hope, telling him that someday his brother would play and talk with him.

My relationship with my husband also suffered. After the massive upheavals of his mother's death, Leo's diagnosis, the move back to DC, and Leo's costly treatment, David and I had no energy left. Our conversations revolved around Lucas's school schedule and Leo's therapy appointments and if we were running low on milk. We didn't see a marriage counselor because we couldn't afford one, and where was the time? David and I did the best we could to stay close as a couple, seeing a movie when we could find a babysitter. I continued to run to maintain my physical and emotional health.

We lived with a mammoth unasked question: Could we continue our financial engineering long enough for Leo to turn the corner? The answer had to be yes. To adjust to the double burden of Leo's expenses and my not working (as in outside the home), David took a job as a financial analyst at an investment research firm. Since we were still sinking, he had to gather his courage and disclose the high cost of Leo's special needs, and the firm generously and amazingly built a theoretical annual bonus amount into his biweekly paycheck. The income—and the skyrocketing value of the house—made it possible to take out a home equity line, which we used to cover Leo's therapy and schooling.

When I looked into the mirror, it reflected a woman I no longer knew. My brow was creased, and a look of introspection replaced innocence in my eyes. I thought about how I would remake my life when Leo's intensive therapy and the money stresses ended, if they ever did end. Ironically, the socially isolated person I tried to keep Leo from becoming was the person I had become. I clung to my only remaining true girlfriend, who lived in Aspen. Other friends dropped away, some treating me and my "special needs" child as if we both had leprosy.

Leo entered his second year of therapy amid a chaotic collision of events. First, Sandra Mailman, our lawyer, informed us that she did not think we had a strong enough case to win reimbursement at due process for Leo's private therapy and schooling for the previous year. Sandra convinced us that the school system could successfully argue that the Janney Pre-K program met the federal test of being "appropriate," because the law didn't entitle Leo to the best education, just an adequate one. We could possibly win reimbursement for the speech-language summer program, which amounted to $3,860. She also recommended that we leave out the cost of the JCC camp since it was not therapeutic. To carry our case forward, we'd have to put at risk more than $10,000 in professional fees.

"Let's do it," I said. Disgusted with the process, we also told Sandra we planned to bypass the educational planning process the following year, even though this created more financial sacrifice for us. Sandra opposed that idea, but I had had enough of listening to school officials dissect my son's deficits like a specimen laid out for an anatomy class, especially if there was little upside.

The next ball to juggle dealt with choosing a private school for Leo to attend for the next school year, which was to begin in fall

2004 when he was five years old. The private school admissions scramble, which started the fall before enrollment, required me to think that far ahead. Leo was in his last year at St. Columba's two-year preschool program, and I wanted to believe that Leo would remain in a regular school with no aide once he left. We planned to hold him back to give him another year to grow socially and emotionally, but not at St. Columba's and not at Janney. This put us in a position of applying to kindergarten programs, which—in DC—get the largest and most competitive pool of applicants.

I knew that the start of Leo's primary school education was probably the most critical crossroads in his development and spent hours strategizing on how to accomplish his acceptance into a regular school. Private schools will take children who receive speech and OT, but they don't want children with special needs (read: disruptive behaviors) because they lack staff to give one child so much attention. Teachers are not always trained to handle behaviors that might include frequent biting and hitting, which are not uncommon traits among children on the spectrum. Leo had never been a behavior problem, and I believed that he could fit in. Admittedly, I wanted to believe this and needed to believe this and so, of course, I believed it.

Dr. Wieder, Leo's child psychologist, recommended Lowell, qualifying her advice with, "But it's hard to get in." She said Lowell understood children like Leo and helped them learn how to recognize and work through frustration. It respected, even celebrated, a child's individual differences, not only in race, ethnicity, and socioeconomic class, but in learning style as well. But I'd have to find a way to describe Leo's challenges. Using the standard euphemism "special needs" would strike him off the list. At Leo's last visit to Yale, nearly a year ago, Dr. Volkmar had looked me in the eye and very pointedly told me, "Leo has more in common with typically developing children than he does with autistic ones." All the Yale experts crowded into the small room had nodded in agreement.

In mid-December, amid all the chaos, we flew to New Haven

again for what would be Leo's third and last evaluation at Yale. The evaluation went as well as it could. Despite his deficits—troublesome eye contact and rigidity—he knocked the answers out of the park. His expressive language had flourished. He scored in the superior range and made the most gains with his ability to manipulate his hands to perform fine-motor tasks. On the intelligence test he scored an eighty-eight, which was somewhat worrisome to me because of the wide discrepancy between his verbal skills and his ability to solve problems with his eyes and mind. A discrepancy of more than fifteen points can signal a learning disability; the difference between Leo's verbal and nonverbal scores was twenty-five points. Again, they discouraged medications to tame his emotions and recommended a Functional Behavioral Assessment, a process to identify the root cause of problem behaviors and to develop interventions for them.

Four days later we passed through metal detectors to sit in the hot seat for our due-process hearing at the DC Office of Special Education. After a late start to our hearing, the hearing officer steered the direction of the case into clear focus. She zeroed in on the part of Leo's educational program that dealt with keeping him in a classroom with nondisabled children.

A representative of the school district rambled on about how the educational planning process works and how summer school services are delivered in the District of Columbia. The hearing officer cut him off before he could finish and moved to end the hearing, handing us another victory in a case that never should have gone to "trial."

Riding high on that triumph, I tried to game the private school acceptance system as much as I could, but there just weren't very many ways to give us an advantage unless the school saw us as a future benefactor. All the schools we toured advertised themselves as gateways to riches and success. Their brochures displayed colorful pictures of lush grounds, expansive libraries, and alumni with

Ivy League degrees, Nobel prizes, Olympic medals, and every other accolade imaginable.

Since I really had no idea what I'd do if we didn't get in somewhere, I was constantly on edge. I was never comfortable knowing that the people I was sizing up were sizing me up, too, asking if Leo fit in, and if my husband and I were genuinely "People Like Us."

However, the process of applying quickly became routine—the tour, generally an interview, and the audition, which for some reason in our epoch is called a "play session." Taking Leo to these play sessions would become a misery of dread before, panic during, and a lingering anxiety afterward. They made my stomach roil with knots.

Not all of the interviews, however, went according to plan. At a private school in Montgomery County, the admission's officer asked routine questions, and we gave our standard replies until I turned to David. He was laughing uncontrollably, trying without success to bring himself under control. I didn't see what was funny, and the interviewer decided to just keep it moving along. David pulled it together, but couldn't bring himself to speak for the rest of the interview. I thanked the woman as she showed us the door. I looked apologetic, and she looked at me with pity. Outside, I glared at David. "What in hell happened to you in there?" "I'm sorry," he said, "but somehow from the Metro to the school and then into the admissions office then into the interview, I hadn't actually looked at you. When I looked for the first time in there and saw you'd dyed your hair trailer park red, I was so startled I started to laugh, and then I just couldn't stop." David looked at me, expecting to be forgiven. "He's not going to get in, is he?" he said. I just started the car. I didn't think my hair was *that* red.

Visiting the Lowell School allowed me to see a slice of kid heaven. This was the school that had turned Leo down two years earlier when I had disclosed his diagnosis in an email message. Now, I was back, with an improved version of Leo. I assumed that no one remembered that email but me. Perched on the crest of a hill, the majestic-looking school was situated on eight bucolic acres next to Rock Creek Park. Whatever lay inside, it was clear that the Lowell grounds had curb appeal.

We applied. To prepare Leo for his play session, scheduled in early January 2004, Dr. Wieder urged me to increase the playdates. She said they would be good practice. Playing with other children did not come naturally to Leo. Dr. Wieder explained that socialization skills begin before children say their first words, and parents shouldn't wait for their children to develop oral communication skills before starting playdates. Babies and toddlers benefit from being in each other's company during the early years because they learn language through gestures. I saw the fault in my decision to keep playdates to a minimum until Leo could talk. How did I miss this?

I had a full battle plan on how to execute a playdate. I'd invite a playmate over and set the kids to mixing potions in a big bowl using old spices, cornstarch, flour, sugar, eggs, chocolate syrup, baking soda, vinegar, and food coloring. I'd tell Leo when it was time to let the other child take a turn and model appropriate language for him. Sometimes, while mixing potions, squirting food coloring got out of hand. I'd say just a "few drops," but Leo would squirt the whole damn bottle and then the other child would pick another color and do the same thing. Then they'd dump an entire box of baking soda and jug of vinegar into the bowl, causing a massive explosion. They had fun, interacting, like normal kids, and when Leo played well, I felt like singing hallelujah.

Other times, when I couldn't engage Leo and his friend, I gave up and hid upstairs. An hour for a playdate was torture when each child went to a separate room to play. After a few playdates, I began to hire students to facilitate. I was always Leo's first choice for a playmate—I was almost always more accommodating than a peer—but my presence changed Leo's behavior. I couldn't be there if he was to get the needed skills from the experience. I relished the chances I had to drop Leo off at another child's house, but I was anxious to learn how it went.

Searching for Acceptance

On the day of his play session at Lowell, in January 2004, we gathered in the lobby with the other parents wearing awkward smiles. As a teacher led us into a large room, a moment of panic seized me. I wondered whether it was worth the discomfort of pushing Leo's own envelope to get him here. "Parents," the teacher declared, "take a deep breath. We're here to have fun. I'd like for you to let your children explore the bookcases. They're free to choose whatever they want and bring it back to the table."

The Lowell teachers walked around the room, saying nothing, but scribbling notes on clipboards as though they were absorbing a college lecture. We were on display for everyone to observe and record, much like fish in an aquarium. "And then they went zoom, zoom, zoom," said Leo, reaching up, holding his little piggies. *Oh, did they catch that interaction?* I looked around, but none of the teachers was in the vicinity to see. *Would he do something again that they could record with a favorable stroke?* I participated in Leo's story, but my stomach knotted with anxiety, and I kept casting my eyes to the other tables, reeling in what looked to be positive play sessions. Leo's thoughts snagged on the pig story, and he stuck to me, refusing to engage with the other children who sought him out to play.

When the play session ended, Leo didn't want to go, saying "I don't want to leave" over and over. I tried to put a positive spin on this with the teachers by saying that he was having a good time.

But Leo repeated "I don't want to leave" enough times for it to be disturbing.

I'd been managing Leo for two and a half years now, and I knew some tricks. "I have a Hershey's chocolate bar in the car," I told him. That allowed him to shift gears, and we made it out the door. This was perhaps not the best strategy to use because now I had to make good on my promise and produce a chocolate candy bar. But I knew what was at stake, and if he was going to blow up, I wanted it to be when he was safely in the car.

I had spent lavishly on application fees, enrolling him in eight schools (including the lottery for a DC charter school), as if I were putting chips on many roulette numbers. But in mid-March, every school except for Grace Episcopal Day School rejected Leo. David supported Leo's going there since it turned out to be our only choice. I called the next day to accept but vowed to try again next fall. There were three other schools on my list, and I didn't want to give up on Lowell.

Leo, five years old, entered Grace as a preschooler after Labor Day 2004, and the search for private schools repeated with the same predictability as the skip on a broken record. This year, however, Lowell wasn't an option because it appeared that it wasn't going to lose any students through attrition for kindergarten.

Lucas moved up to second grade and continued in Janney's after-care program until he started to complain, and guilty as I was about not giving him more attention, I caved in to his request to take him out. Leo, meanwhile, adjusted well to his new school. He developed a friendship with Hannah, a little blond girl. Their teacher said they played well together, sharing an interest in science and big words. Leo talked about her at home, and it thrilled me that Leo was making a friend—a major milestone in his social development.

The fall passed, and I breathed easier. No due-process hearing to prepare for and no Yale evaluation. We applied to three schools for Leo. Each had everything David and I wanted—small class sizes, nonsectarian environments, and challenging yet homelike environments. Leo also took the Wechsler Preschool and Primary Scale of Intelligence (WPPSI, pronounced "whip-see") test again. This time his score leaped from average to on the cusp of superior intelligence, with no difference in performance between his verbal and nonverbal (problem-solving) scores. How he had closed the twenty-five point gap in a year astounded me.

In February, we received Leo's reenrollment forms from Grace. Since we wouldn't hear back from the other schools until March, we filled them out and paid a $700 nonrefundable deposit. Grace's kindergarten program was full day, doubling the tuition to about $14,000 a year.

UGLY BIRTHDAY PARTY

Around the same time Leo received an invitation to celebrate Hannah's fifth birthday—one of those milestones parents celebrate with the same fervor and grandiosity of a child's first.

A few weeks before Hannah's party, her mother, Melissa, had invited Leo over for a playdate. I stayed and saw how well the children interacted. Near the end, however, Leo got frustrated with magnetized building blocks, blurting out, "This sucks!" Melissa tried, unconvincingly, to brush off the remark by saying, "Hannah doesn't even know what that means," but her demeanor said "suck" was a four-letter word Hannah had never heard. Despite that, Melissa invited Leo to Hannah's birthday party. Leo was excited, and I chose a gift costing more than the usual to show Melissa I cared about her daughter's friendship with Leo.

The morning of the party, we arrived a bit early. Melissa ushered Leo and Hannah into the basement and fixed me a cup of coffee. I offered to help, but she said she could handle the last-minute preparations. The other children soon started to arrive. Leo emerged from the basement, confused at seeing his classmates from Grace, perhaps thinking this was a playdate, not a birthday party. We had discussed the party in advance, a technique called "priming," going over who would be there and what to expect. Leo had an excellent auditory memory, and I thought he had understood.

I intervened by taking Leo back to the basement before he had an outburst. I didn't want the other parents to see him complain in the presence of their children. I heard Dr. Wieder's voice reminding what to do in circumstances like this: *Ask him an intelligent question. It gets him to stop and think.* But the thought remained in my head.

The children tearing up and down the stairs seemed to frazzle Melissa, who tried to contain them in the basement with an arts-and-crafts activity. The children stuck gold and red stars on their magic hats, but Leo had no interest in stickers. Then I realized that the magic hats announced the theme of the party and I had not prepared Leo for a magic show. But he'd like magic. All kids like magic.

Melissa called the children to the living room for the magician, the Great Zucchini. Leo preferred to stay in the basement until I coaxed him upstairs and he found a spot to sit. When the magician asked for a volunteer, the children waved their hands and called, "Me! Me! Me!" Leo was always a few seconds behind in raising his hand, if he raised it all, and then he cautiously pointed his hand upward with hesitation, as if he were testing the temperature of water. Time after time, the Great Zucchini passed over Leo for a more exuberant child. Leo's face tightened. "It's no big deal" was echoing in my head.

Another fifteen minutes passed, and Leo did not get called on. When the show ended, Leo scrunched his eyes and nose together, which meant he was about to cry. The other children dashed out of the room to eat cake in the dining room. I rushed in to ask the magician, "Could you please do a magic trick with my son?"

He happily complied, pulling out a small red foam ball from his pocket. The ball vanished from the magician's hand and reappeared behind Leo's ear. Leo's face relaxed. "I want to do all the magic tricks," he said.

"Oh, Leo, that's not possible," I said.

Leo's face crumbled, and he started to cry. I freaked. *Think fast. Get Leo away from the other children.* I edged him to the stairway and I followed him up to the second-floor landing. "Happy Birthday" was going on without us downstairs. I tried to comfort him, get him to stop crying, to stop embarrassing me. I didn't know what else to do but move into the bathroom. Before I could, Melissa loomed in the hallway, looking at me as if I had just splattered ketchup on her favorite white blouse. "I think you'd better leave," she said. "I don't want you to ruin Hannah's birthday party."

My mouth fell open but no words came out as I struggled to process what she had said. *Did I just hear you say my child's tears were ruining your daughter's birthday party?* I was stunned, mortified, confused, hurt, defeated. *If I could just get to the bathroom, another four feet to the right, and close the door.*

"Yes," I said, shifting my gaze back and forth between her and Leo, trying to communicate nonverbally that I'd like to calm him down first. Melissa left, and I looked at Leo, still crying incessantly. I rubbed Leo's back. "Leo, don't cry," I said gently, dropping to my knees, nudging him closer to the bathroom. "Please, Leo, calm down. It will be all right. Mommy loves you."

Suddenly, Melissa was back. "Jayne, you need to leave," she said. "Do you want me to get your coat? I'll put your coat and goodie bag on the steps."

I was so angry I wanted to pull out her hair. *You bitch! What do you want me to do? Grab my sobbing child and run out the front door?* Although screaming at her would just have multiplied my problems—two wild cave moms going at each other—the deep recesses of my brain gave it fleeting consideration. She left again, and I pulled Leo into the bathroom, closing the door, reassuring him that he'd be all right.

He stopped crying but was emotionally unstable and fragile. "Leo, do you want to go downstairs and eat some cake?"

We held hands down the stairs and sat at the dining room table, now vacant and strewn with party favors and cake crumbs. I cut Leo a piece of cake, rubbing his back some more. Another mother asked me if I was okay. "Melissa told us to leave," I said, drawing short choppy breaths. "She said Leo was ruining Hannah's party." Then she rubbed *my* back and invited me to meet her for coffee.

The other mothers were outside watching their children break a piñata. As they drifted back in and asked me what happened, I repeated Melissa's callous remark, seeking sympathy. Probably embarrassed, they kept their distance from me.

As the party wound down, Melissa avoided looking at me. She said she'd call to apologize. I nodded. When she called, her apology was perfunctory. She admitted to insensitivity, but I knew she blamed me for not running for the car in shame, like you'd whisk a crying baby out of a theater.

I knew she'd never let her daughter play with Leo again. She poured herself into the illusion of creating a perfect household and raising perfect children, and Leo had ruined that illusion for her. While I could forgive Melissa, I could not forget.

From that day I yearned to get out of Grace so that I didn't have to face those parents. I wasn't exactly ostracized, but I never again felt welcome. Perhaps it was just my own embarrassment that didn't go away, but I now joined David in the feeling that we didn't belong.

In March 2005, we got our response from the schools, and again Leo was rejected, though he made the wait list at one.

Making the Grade

I felt encouraged when Leo's March report showed continued progress:

> Leo continues to bring lively interests and inventive energy to our Pre-Kindergarten class. He is passionate about his ideas for imaginative play . . . and his ideas often stimulate his playmates to make suggestions of their own. . . . Leo's strong language skills continue to grow. He enjoys riddles, tongue twisters and . . . jokes. Leo speaks in complex sentences, asks and answers questions in detail, and uses comparative words to express his observations related to number, size, and weight. In P.E., Leo is willing to try new challenges and increasingly willing to keep trying when his first attempt is not successful. One day, for example, Mrs. Mann demonstrated how to swing a rope overhead with one hand, while galloping like a cowboy. Leo persisted with great concentration (and some grumbling) until he figured out, first of all, how to gather the tail of the rope in his other hand to keep from tripping on it, then how to swing the rope while running, and finally how to coordinate the galloping gait with his swinging arm.

His teacher highlighted Leo's intelligences, taken from Howard Gardener's 1993 book, *Frames of Mind*, which introduced the theory of multiple intelligences. Leo's strengths were linguistic and spatial. He was sensitive to the meaning and order of words like a writer or lawyer, and he possessed the ability to manipulate space (as in the visual arts) like a sculptor or architect.

As Leo's world unfolded before him, my world finally closed in on me. Because of irregular payments, our maxed-out credit cards stopped working, which disturbed me, but the denial of my debit card floored me. I began to figure out just how much debt we had taken on. Leo's therapeutic expenses and my missing salary had cost us well over $100,000 each year for the past three. And this on top of bad business decisions David made that added to our burden. Would we toss our car into the ever-widening maw of debt? Our house was at risk next, and losing that would be a blow from which we would never recover.

Just before Memorial Day, a mom friend told me Lowell had an opening for its kindergarten program. I never thought I'd hear those words. I jumped on this inside knowledge. I called the school to confirm the opening, drove there to pick up the application, and drove back to hand-deliver the completed paperwork. I followed up with a phone call. The school needed Leo's progress reports from Grace, and they scheduled a play session.

Two weeks passed, and no word from Lowell. Something was wrong. I called and found out Grace wouldn't send over Leo's progress reports because of an unresolved "financial issue." That had to mean the first tuition payment we had delayed because of our financial crisis. David called Lowell, asking if we could send the progress reports ourselves. The school agreed, and we were one step closer to leaving Grace.

Days later, Lowell called. Leo got in. At last. A break. Then, another loss.

After David met with a credit counselor, we realized that we had to file for bankruptcy. As we sought a bankruptcy attorney, we signed Leo's $19,500 tuition contract for Lowell.

On July 11, 2005, I withdrew Leo from Grace and hoped that the school would not come after us for the tuition we had agreed to pay. The head of the school called and reminded me of our obligation, but the school did not pursue the matter.

I was smothered in stress and feared becoming homeless. On a morning run, I stopped to talk to a homeless woman. Hers was a world too horrid to contemplate joining. I searched for a job and found one and started within one week after we filed for bankruptcy on July 28.

Over the next six months, the broken and disjointed parts of our lives began to slowly reassemble themselves into some kind of order. My first paycheck allowed us to make Leo's first tuition payment at Lowell, and we were discharged of all our debts and allowed to keep the house and car. Despite the bankruptcy, our lives had evolved to a better place: Leo found joy, which gave us all a reason to celebrate. In my world, we were almost normal.

TWO

▶▶▶ Something's Not Right: Warning Signs

After Leo turned one, I had hoped that he'd come to me when I called out his name. But he just went about his baby business. I had no idea that his lack of responsiveness signaled that my son was at high risk for autism. I kept thinking that he was too immature to understand. Another ten months passed, his behavior hadn't changed, and his speech didn't evolve. Neither my husband, David, nor I could construct a coherent profile about Leo's development, but a chalky outline had begun to emerge.

I wanted a clearer sign; it was David who got one. It happened the day he took Leo to Green Lakes State Park, near Syracuse. The park surrounds a deep lake the aquamarine color of the Caribbean that was created by a waterfall when the glaciers receded. David took him there on a spring morning before Memorial Day, a few weeks before the swimmers and crowds poured in. A breeze blew from the south, just strong enough to rattle the branches and displace the last remaining dry leaves from the trees.

Leo was just short of his second birthday, and David expected that he'd do more or less what Lucas had done at the beach when he was two—run, get his feet wet, chase seagulls, throw some rocks into the water, dig in the sand. But Leo ignored the sand toys and everything around him. Instead, he rested on his knees, pressed his forehead into the wet sand at the shoreline, and then dribbled handfuls of sand onto the sides of his head. At first, David laughed at Leo's antics. Then his behavior started to disturb him, so he spoke to Leo gently and tried to redirect him.

"Leo, let's build a sandcastle," said David.

Leo picked up another glob of sand and released it on his temples.

"Look, Leo," said David as he turned a bucket of sand upside down to build a tower. "Help me. Here's the bucket. You try."

But Leo ignored David as if he were deaf. David glanced over his shoulder to see if anyone was watching. He shifted his body to shelter Leo's behavior from the crowd of sunbathers behind him.

David then picked Leo up, cleaned him off, and took him far from the shore. As soon as David put him down, Leo ran back to the edge of the water, back to the same position with his forehead half buried, dropping wet sand onto his temples.

"Leo, stop, stop doing that," David said. "Play with me." But the words did not register with Leo.

Twice more, David overpowered Leo and tried to redirect him. Twice more, he failed. Stunned and confused, he sat there watching Leo. This was more than just curious; it was a sign that something was very wrong, something that would have to be analyzed, diagnosed, corrected, and overcome. Our son was burying his head in the sand. What were we missing?

That night, we poured ourselves a drink, and David related what had happened, characterizing it as his "oh, fuck" moment.

I never had an "oh, fuck" moment. I kept believing that everything was okay, and for a while longer, it seemed as if it was. Words would occasionally pop out of Leo's mouth. In the car, he said "truck." When I turned to look out the side window, sure enough I saw a truck drive by. I felt relieved. He *can* associate words with objects. Leo is learning to talk. I can't recall any other words Leo said, however. No mama, dada, or babbling—just words, popping out of his mouth every now and then. In some future time, I would come to realize the deception of this form of abnormal language development.

At home, Leo was obsessed with Thomas the Tank Engine, the blue wooden toy train with a rosy-cheeked face. And not just the one little train itself but the Thomas the Tank Engine videos, clothing, and music that created this immersive environment. Leo didn't talk to us, but he'd stand beside the train table rolling the trains over the same spot and squatting down to see the wheels at eye level, muttering to himself as if he were directing a play. Sometimes, he lined up his trains with the precision of a ruler. But Leo ignored Lucas and excluded me from his play, no matter how I tried to join in.

After twenty minutes or so of playing with his trains, he'd abruptly leave, tearing down the long hallway to our bedroom, where he would stop in one place, spinning and raising his arms. David called it Leo's "little dance." I would follow him into the room and watch as Leo's feet traced the floral design on the Oriental rug, pacing as if he were trying to figure something out. Not once did he raise his head, even if I called his name. Then he would run back to the train table, picking up where he had left off.

As more weeks passed, David and I both noticed his lack of responsiveness. To test his hearing, we clapped loudly from behind him. When Leo flinched, it refuted, in our opinion, that Leo couldn't hear. We also observed that when we had something he wanted, we could get his attention—even if he were lost on the island of Sodor, Thomas's make-believe home. But we didn't yet bring in specialists to observe him and validate our concerns.

Looking back, of course, I realize that we were blind. There were even earlier warning signs. At four months, when I crouched over him in the bouncy seat and shook my head to rouse him for a snapshot, I had to shout his name several times in order to force a smile. With my finger over the shutter, I jiggled the bouncy seat and then tickled him under the armpit, depressing the shutter when he laughed. I framed the photo for display on the fireplace mantel. It shows Leo with a wide open mouth and making eye contact, but the photo op had been a setup.

At the JCC child-care center, his teacher, Erica, said he was "right on track." When we met with her for our parent-teacher conference when Leo was twenty-two months old, she flipped his progress report around so we could read it. All the boxes that covered language and social skills had checkmarks in the satisfactory range. Somehow seeing it in black and white made me more fully aware of how wrong those answers were.

"But he's not playing with other children," I said.

"All children develop differently. He's right on track. I'm telling you, there's nothing wrong with your child."

A few weeks later, when I was on the verge of reaching the conclusion that something might be seriously wrong, I told our pediatrician, Dr. Roberts, during Leo's eighteen-month well-baby checkup that he wasn't talking. Dr. Roberts reassured me that some kids develop slower than others. I failed to mention that Leo didn't express his needs, play with me, or respond to his name.

But I mentioned that Leo could memorize passages from books, songs, and videos and parrot them. I wondered if Leo was a genius because he could clearly articulate the entire text of *Angus Lost*. Although Leo could repeat what he had heard, I couldn't carry on a conversation with him. He wouldn't respond to any question or command. Dr. Roberts shrugged off Leo's memorization skills as not being a developmental milestone.

Given that language explodes after children turn two, Dr. Roberts advised that I wait another six months and reexamine Leo's progress then. He said he knew a developmental pediatrician in town and would call him if my worries persisted. It was a reassuring thought, to wait. But something deep within told me that I had an immediate crisis, and if my pediatrician wasn't going to help me figure it out, then it was up to me.

I had never heard of a developmental pediatrician or the role one played in a child's development. I look back now on how ignorant I was about child development in general and abnormal development in particular. I thought the negative results of my amniocentesis guaranteed me a healthy child. As an older mom, I had worried about Down syndrome and whether Leo would be born with ten toes and ten fingers. The thought that he would have something wrong with his brain was so far removed from my conscious mind that I still have a hard time believing I could have been so stupid not to have thought *that*.

Almost everyone was telling me that there was nothing wrong with Leo. How easy it would have been to rely on their judgment. But I had scrutinized and observed Leo's behavior for months until every fiber of my being resonated with concern. I had a deep inner knowing that allowed my convictions to surface. Inside, a growing sense of urgency and panic engulfed me. Whatever was wrong with Leo, I knew treating it was urgent, whatever "it" was. If Leo's problems had something to do with his brain, could I do something about it? Wasn't the brain malleable at his age? Untrained and unprepared, I felt I was at the start of a marathon that, as far as I knew, didn't have a clearly marked route or visible finish line. My inner voice screamed: Something is wrong with my child. Don't wait any longer.

What Is Autism?

Autism is a mysterious brain disorder with no known cure.

A diagnosis of autism involves a triad of impairments. Think of three angles of a triangle, with each angle representing an impaired skill. At the top is communication, and each of the bottom two angles represents social interaction and behaviors.

To explain further, communication—either verbal or nonverbal—is the essence of how we express our needs and desires. Without this skill, we cannot communicate successfully with another person—neither respond to them nor understand the meaning of gestures, such as something so minor as glancing at a watch to indicate time is running out.

Impaired social interaction hinders our ability to relate to other people—a friend, bank teller, colleague, and so on. Deficient social skills manifest themselves in a variety of ways, from poor eye contact to a lack of empathy to an overall indifference toward others. Impaired behaviors take the form of isolated interests, and repetitive or restricted actions—clapping hands, flapping arms, or something subtle, such as humming. For a triangle to exist, there must be three angles. Similarly, for a diagnosis of autism to exist, it must encompass these three classes of impairments.

But just as the shape of a triangle changes when the measurement of one of its vertices changes, so will the diagnosis of autism. While one child might be diagnosed with classic autism, another might show atypical signs and receive a diagnosis of pervasive developmental disorder–not otherwise specified (PDD–NOS), which is generally considered a milder form of autism but not always. The severity and intensity of impairments vary widely, with different levels of functioning and different compensatory skills, making each child as different as the many faces of a triangle when its vertices change.

But the unifying features for children with an autistic or autism spectrum disorder are that they don't play well with others, make friends, act appropriately, or carry on a spontaneous to-and-fro conversation. Condensed to its core, autism makes rewarding and enjoyable communication and social interaction difficult. It's not that children don't want to communicate and relate socially; it's that most of them can't. They often perceive the world as a place of things rather than people.

Autism experts agree that early intervention works when treatment is delivered at a very young age because it may ultimately lessen the expression of the disorder, inhibit inappropriate patterns of behavior from being established, allow for the teaching of purposeful speech at a decisive time in language development, and give families time to make a healthy adjustment.

It also takes advantage of when the brain is most malleable. At birth, a baby's brain is largely undeveloped, but it is rich with neurons, or nerve cells, containing 100 billion of them, or about the same number as stars in the universe. During a baby's first three years of life, the brain experiences a growth spurt and races to create hundreds of trillions of pathways to connect these neurons, giving the brain its greatest capacity for change, known as its plasticity. These neurons form the framework of a baby's brain and deeply influence whether a baby will be able to engage and develop successful relationships or retreat into a solitary, frightening world.

The simple game of peekaboo, for example, causes the brain to change its physical structure, as thousands of cells respond in a matter of seconds: This game "turns" on some brain cells, creating

▶ **FAST FACT**

Four leading institutions—the American Academy of Pediatrics, the American Academy of Child and Adolescent Psychiatry, the U.S. Surgeon General, and the National Research Council—have called for early intervention for children with autism. But less than 10 percent of children who are afflicted by this disorder receive the recommended twenty-five hours a week of year-round treatment, and when they do receive treatment, the quality varies greatly, according to Dr. Catherine Lord, chairwoman of the committee that wrote the report "Educating Children with Autism."

new connections, and strengthening others. As a child grows older, these favorable circumstances for growth diminish.

That's why it's critically important to intervene early if you suspect an autism spectrum disorder. Whether or not recovery happens, early intervention holds the power to change your child's destiny. It takes tenacity, perseverance, and vigilance—attributes you'll need to manage an early intervention program, which will typically last four to five years. According to the research, your

▶ **INFORM YOURSELF**

To delve deeper into autism spectrum disorders, find a reference book in the psychology section of your local bookstore or go online. The Centers for Disease Control and Prevention's Autism Information Center* and the American Academy of Pediatrics' autism section[†] contain a plethora of information on autism. The National Institute of Mental Health offers a free booklet.[‡]

As you explore other sites, pay attention to the source of information. Much misinformation about autism spectrum disorders and treatments abounds on the Web. Autism Watch,[§] a scientific guide that reviews sites for fraudulent and misleading claims, will help you sort the good from the bad. Searching the Healthfinder service** of the U.S. Department of Health and Human Services and Tufts University's Child and Family Web Guide[††] will produce reliable sites. Healthfinder only lists sites maintained by the U.S. government and select nonprofits, and Tufts experts screen sites for authenticity and credibility. Also look for sites that display the Health on the Net icon. Health on the Net[‡‡] grew out of the United Nations' 1995 initiative to guide Internet users to reliable sources of online healthcare information.

* www.cdc.gov/ncbddd/autism/index.htm
[†] www.medicalhomeinfo.org/health/autism.html
[‡] www.nimh.nih.gov/publicat/autism.cfm#8#8
[§] www.autism-watch.org
** www.healthfinder.gov
[††] www.cfw.tufts.edu
[‡‡] www.hon.ch

child will likely see his greatest gains in the first two years. While not all children will swing open the doors of their public elementary school, don't let ignorance crush hope that your child won't be one of them. Research shows that some children do improve and lose their diagnosis.[1] If you wait to intervene, research shows that intervention costs more and is less effective, but whether or not recovery is an option, it's never too late to start intervention. You can still define important outcomes for your child.

▶ **FAST FACT** ———————————————————————————————

The American Psychiatric Association's *Diagnostic and Statistical Manual of Mental Disorders* (fourth edition, text revision) is the mental health bible that defines the diagnostic criteria used by professionals to diagnose autism spectrum disorders.[2] The *DSM-IV-TR* lists five types of autism spectrum disorders. PDD (pervasive developmental disorder) is not a spectrum disorder but is the umbrella term that they all fall under. They include:

Autism or autistic disorder: Classic autism appears before age three and is characterized by three distinct traits: (1) poor social interaction, (2) lack of communication, both verbal and nonverbal, and (3) odd and repetitive behavior and fixed interests. Four times more common in boys than girls. The disorder develops along two distinct paths: Either symptoms occur early in life or a child develops normally then regresses, losing language and social skills. Added to the *DSM-III* in 1980.

Asperger's disorder: Unlike autism, children with Asperger's disorder show no obvious delay in language or cognitive development. If fact, they can be verbally precocious. Defining characteristics include: social cluelessness, isolated or excessive interest in a topic or object; awkward body movements; sensory issues; and inflexibility. Average age of diagnosis: seven years old.[3] Added to the *DSM-IV* in 1994.

Atypical autism or PDD–NOS: Pervasive developmental disorder–not otherwise specified is a diagnosis given to children who do not quite meet the diagnostic definition for autism but who still have

impairments in the three areas indicated by classic autism, though intellectual impairment is rarer.

Childhood disintegrative disorder: This extremely rare autism spectrum disorder is also known as regressive autism. Only 100 cases have
been reported since 1908. Children develop normally for three to four
years before they experience a pronounced and extensive loss in
skills—motor, language, and social—and bodily functions. Often mis-
diagnosed as autism.

Rett's disorder: This is another rare but severe spectrum disorder that
primarily strikes girls between six and eighteen months. Early signs
include loss of speech and motor skills. Hand wringing is a common
trait. Unlike most of the other autism spectrum disorders, it is caused
by mutations in a single gene.

The Childbrain.com site of pediatric neurology excerpts the PDD diagnostic criteria from the *DSM-IV-TR*. Choose "PDD/Autism" from the
menu bar. For a child to receive a diagnosis of autism, the child must
show six or more of twelve symptoms across the three main areas.
The Early Intervention Network has translated the *DSM-IV* diagnostic
criteria for autism and related disorders in layman's terms.*

* www.actearly.org/dsmIV

◄ PRACTICAL ADVICE ►

You play a pivotal role in influencing your child's development if
the signs of an autism spectrum disorder appear.

You can take many steps in the process toward helping your
child participate as fully in life as possible. Educating yourself to
make informed decisions about how best to help your child is the
first step. Let's begin.

Is There Something Wrong with Your Child?

When you're going through the discovery phase of understanding what might be wrong with your child, it's natural for you to have conflicting emotions, disturbing thoughts, and unanswered questions. Your instincts tell you that whatever might be wrong could be serious. You keep thinking about behaviors that bother you and rationalize why things will be okay. You may even feel that the grieving process has begun, even though you cannot put your finger squarely on the source of your sorrow. Stop thinking. Pick up the phone. You need to answer the question: Is there something wrong with my child? Ask it.

Calling your pediatrician is a natural first step. You selected your pediatrician because you trust her advice and judgment, and you may assume she's trained to screen your child for a developmental problem, but don't count on it. Office visits miss 70 percent of children with developmental and behavioral problems, according to ForePath Ltd., an online developmental and behavioral screening service used by professionals and parents to screen children for autism spectrum disorders and other disabilities.

The practice of early screening for delays in social and emotional development during well-baby checkups is fairly new and not yet a regular part of all doctors' routines. But the American Academy of Pediatrics wants to change that. In October 2007, it issued new guidelines that recommend formal screening for all U.S. children by age two. During your child's checkup, if you think something is

▶ **FAST FACT**

Studies have found that parents of children later diagnosed with an autism spectrum disorder typically notice something wrong with their child's development at around fifteen months but don't raise their concerns until much later.

wrong (after all, you are the closest observer of your child's behavior and the best person to notice a potential problem), you should, in a friendly but persistent manner, raise your concerns and insist on a developmental screening.

Initial Screening

Developmental screening tools are as important as the height and weight measurements your pediatrician charts on well-baby check-ups. They focus on your baby's social and emotional milestones. Like physical development, social and emotional development also brings many firsts—first smile, first wave, first imitation, first idea. These milestones are sometimes harder to pinpoint than the signs of physical growth. But like the inches on a growth chart, they are measures of how your child relates socially and handles emotions compared with his or her peers. These milestones evolve and deepen in complexity as children age.

Although all children are unique and come from different backgrounds that influence their pace of development, style of communication, and the way they react to people and the larger world, all children progress through an identifiable sequence of physical, cognitive, and emotional growth and change.

According to infant specialist Dr. Stanley Greenspan, children move through six stages of emotional growth that lead to symbolic

▶ **FAST FACT** ───────────────────────────────────

The simple test of calling out your baby's name to see if he responds could lead to an earlier diagnosis of an autism spectrum disorder. Researchers say that babies who don't respond to their name by their first birthday are more likely to be diagnosed with ASD or other developmental problem by age two.

thinking and orchestrate a child's development in other capacities. (See Table 1, "How Babies Develop a Social Brain.") When these milestones do not occur, developmental problems, including autism, arise.

The path to discovering that something is awry with your child is different for every parent, but the signs that define autism spectrum disorders are the same. They are not always present at birth, as once thought. However, within the first year if it's hard to get a smile out of your baby, you should worry. Vocal patterns that go on and on and squeals where the quality of the tone seems odd also could signal trouble. A cardinal feature of autism, for example, is a lack of joint attention, which develops around nine months of age and involves a baby's ability to mutually share enjoyment about another person or object with a spontaneous shift in eye gaze from person to object and back to person. The development of this skill is critical to more complex social behavior. There are other early warning signs. (See Table 2, "The Earliest Signs of Autism: When to Worry.")

Many of the warning signs involve a baby's social and emotional growth. A test doctors use to check this growth in babies as young as one month and up to age forty-two months is the third edition of the Bayley Scales of Infant Development. The Bayleys-III also measures motor and mental growth. The social-emotional component includes a short parent questionnaire that was developed by Dr. Greenspan.

▶ **FAST FACT** ───────────────────────────────

The Centers for Disease Control and Prevention reports that the average age for an autism spectrum disorder diagnosis in most states is four years old or later.* According to a study of children on Medicaid, African-Americans aren't diagnosed until they are nearly eight years old, while Latino children on average don't get diagnosed until they're almost nine.[4]

* www.cdc.gov/ncbddd/autism/documents/autismcommunityreport.pdf

HOW BABIES DEVELOP A SOCIAL BRAIN

Healthy Development	What It Means	Questions to Ask Now
Shared attention and emotional regulation (0–3 months)	Many subtle back-and-forth emotional interactions and ability to self-soothe in response to sights, sounds, touch, movement, and other sensory experiences.	1. How do you feel about the way your baby looks at you? 2. Does your baby look toward you when you talk or smile, or when you give him other interesting looks? 3. How do you feel about the way you are able to help your baby calm down? Are you able to calm your baby?
Engaging and relating (2–5 months)	Develops emotional and intimate relationships with caregivers.	1. How do you feel about your relationship with your baby? 2. Is your baby usually happy and smiling and making interesting sounds when she sees you?
Purposeful, two-way emotional interactions (4–10 months)	Initiating and responding with back-and-forth interactions involving a range of gestures and sounds: cooing, head nodding, turning to look.	
Back-and-forth emotional signaling and shared social problem solving (10–18 months)	Solving problems through many social and emotional interactions in a row.	1. How do you feel about the way your baby or toddler interacts with you? 2. Does your baby initiate interactions with sounds or smiles and then respond with more sounds and smiles after you respond? 3. Does your baby look at you for decisions? 4. Does your toddler (12–18 months) show you what he wants and try to get your help?

continues on next page . . .

Table 1

Healthy Development	What It Means	Questions to Ask Now
		5. Does your toddler take delight in showing you a toy or favorite picture in a book?
		6. Does your toddler come to you for support?
Creating emotionally meaningful symbols and words (18–30 months)	Meaningful use of ideas and words to express ideas in pretend play or real-life situations.	1. How do you feel about the way your child uses words or ideas?
		2. Does she use words to let you know what she wants or to share her feelings?
		3. Does he engage in pretend play (feeding a doll)?
		4. Does she use several ideas in a row in a way that makes sense to you? (30–48 months)
		5. Does he ask questions, such as "Where is the truck going?"
Building logical bridges between meaningful ideas (30–42 months)	Connecting ideas logically.	

Source: *Engaging Autism: Using the Floortime Approach to Help Children Relate, Communicate, and Think*, by Stanley I. Greenspan, MD, and Serena Wieder, PhD. Centers for Disease Control and Prevention/Interdisciplinary Council on Developmental Learning Disorders: Collaboration Report on a Framework for Early Identification and Preventive Intervention of Emotional and Developmental Challenges

THE EARLIEST SIGNS OF AUTISM: WHEN TO WORRY

By 6 months*	By 14 months	By 24 months
No eye contact with parents	No single words or no attempt to say a consonant and vowel to form a word	Does not initiate 2-word phrases (a noun and verb)
No cooing or babbling	Not pointing or waving	Imitation does not develop
No vocal turn-taking (baby makes a sound, adult makes a sound)	No response when name is called	No pretend play
Not responding to peekaboo	Indifferent to others	No interest in peers
No smiling when parents smile	Repetitive behaviors: moving car back & forth, persistent rocking, frequent hand flapping	
	Fixation on a single object	
	Oversensitivity to textures, smells, sounds	
	Strong resistance to change in routine	
	Any loss of language or social skill	

ANY LOSS OF LANGUAGE OR SKILL AT ANY AGE

Source: Rebecca Landa, PhD, Center for Autism and Related Disorders at the Kennedy Krieger Institute, Baltimore.
*Skills are cumulative, meaning if 6-month skills are not present by 14 months, it still is a cause for concern.

Table 2

One of the most popular screening tools for autism is the M-CHAT (Modified Checklist for Autism in Toddlers) parent questionnaire. The M-CHAT is a series of twenty-three yes-or-no questions that focus primarily on a child's language and social skills. The M-CHAT *screens* for the possibility of an autism spectrum disorder in children as young as sixteen months.

You can take the M-CHAT online for a small fee ($9.95) at the Forepath site.* The M-CHAT is the second of two tests given, with the first being the ten-question PEDS, or Parents' Evaluation of Development Status. Both the American Academy of Pediatrics and the American Academy of Neurology have identified these screening tools as accurate and valid. The test is taken online and requires only a few minutes to complete; the scoring is automated, and parents can print out the findings in the form of a referral letter to show to their pediatrician. The letter also includes insurance reimbursement codes.

▶ **FAST FACT** ———————————————————————————

Many screening tools rely on your responses to simple yes-or-no questions. A professional also may observe your child. Key questions include: Does your child point or play imaginatively? Children who cannot play symbolically are at a high risk for autism. It is essential to understand that screening instruments are not diagnostic tools. These tools help determine whether further testing is required. First Signs, a nonprofit focused on early identification and intervention of children with developmental delays and disorders, has compiled a list of recommended screening tools for autism spectrum disorders.[†]

[†] www.firstsigns.org/screening/tools/rec.htm

* www.forepath.org

M-CHAT:
Modified Checklist for Autism in Toddlers

Please fill out the following about how your child usually is. Please try to answer every question. If the behavior is rare (e.g., you've seen it once or twice), *please answer as if the child does not do it.*

1. Does your child enjoy being swung, bounced on your knee, etc.?   YES   NO

2. Does your child take an interest in other children?   YES   NO

3. Does your child like climbing on things, such as stairs?   YES   NO

4. Does your child enjoy playing peekaboo/hide-and-seek?   YES   NO

5. Does your child ever pretend, for example, to talk on the phone or take care of a doll or pretend other things?   YES   NO

6. Does your child ever use his index finger to point, to ask for something?   YES   NO

7. Does your child ever use her index finger to point, to indicate interest in something?   YES   NO

8. Can your child play properly with toys (e.g., cars or bricks) without just mouthing, fiddling, or dropping them?   YES   NO

9. Does your child ever bring objects over to you (parent) to show you something?   YES   NO

10. Does your child look you in the eye for more than a second or two?   YES   NO

11. Does your child ever seem oversensitive to noise (e.g., plugging ears)?   YES   NO

12. Does your child smile in response to your face or your smile?   YES   NO

13. Does your child imitate you? (e.g., you make a face—will your child imitate it?)   YES   NO

14. Does your child respond to his name when you call?   YES   NO

15. If you point at a toy across the room, does your child look at it?   YES   NO

16. Does your child walk?   YES   NO

17. Does your child look at things you are looking at?   YES   NO

18. Does your child make unusual finger movements near her face?   YES   NO

19. Does your child try to attract your attention to his own activity?   YES   NO

20. Have you ever wondered if your child is deaf?   YES   NO

21. Does your child understand what people say?   YES   NO

22. Does your child sometimes stare at nothing or wander with no purpose?   YES   NO

23. Does your child look at your face to check your reaction when faced with something unfamiliar?   YES   NO

Have you ever filled out this form for this child before?   YES   NO

If you decide to take these tests, answer the questions honestly. The rule of thumb for scoring the M-CHAT is that the more questions a child "fails," the more at risk the child is for an autism spectrum disorder. It is critical to note that the person taking the M-CHAT is not meant to score it. So, if you take the test on paper and see many red flags, call your pediatrician. You cannot rely on your judgment as proof that there either is—or isn't—something wrong with your child. If there is one thing about human nature, it's that we want to portray ourselves in a more favorable image than reality suggests. That also holds true for our children. No one wants to describe their child's negative behaviors or poor play and social skills. But to admit to the truth puts your child on a path to becoming the best he can be.

▶ **INFORM YOURSELF** ———————————————————————————

A free publication developed by the Colorado Autism Task Force, *Early Identification and Intervention for The Spectrum of Autism** contains a detailed chart that lists early warning signs, broken down by age, for screening under the categories "Sensory-Motor," "Speech-Language," and "Social and Emotional Growth." You can also go to the homepage of the site† and search for the publication using the keywords "autism task force" (no quotes). Look for the publication's name in the search results.

* www.cde.state.co.us/cdesped/download/pdf/Early_Ident_Invert4Autism-printable.pdf
† www.cde.state.co.us

THREE

▶ ▶ ▶ Evaluation and Diagnosis

My first experience with getting a diagnosis was the equivalent of brutal shock therapy, but it didn't have to be. I panicked and pushed my pediatrician to call a developmental pediatrician. My pediatrician told me I could jump ahead of the six-month waiting list if I would agree to skip a full-team evaluation. I didn't bother to ask what that meant or realize the mistake I was about to make. I felt as if he'd done me a favor, and I grabbed the appointment as a result of my compelling urge to know as soon as possible what was wrong with Leo. That evaluation, however, propelled me to a second evaluation within four months that not only modified the result but, just as importantly, provided some concrete guidance on what to do next.

Days before the first evaluation, I prepared myself by reading a trifold brochure from the doctor's office. It summarized in three short bullet points the triad of impairments related to autism—poor social skills, poor verbal skills, and odd behaviors. My mind wrestled with these criteria, but I could not, would not, pronounce my son autistic.

· The First Evaluation

The evaluation room lacked the symmetry and precision of a clinical setting. The couch and chairs were skewed at strange angles, as if an unexpected disaster had forced someone to suddenly abandon arranging them. It was September 4, 2001, a week before the United States was shocked into a period of fear and anxiety.

David, Leo, and I waited here for Dr. Sherman, a shorter-than-average man with hair of Einstein proportions, to begin the evaluation. When he arrived with his nurse, he slouched forward in his swivel chair and started asking questions.

"When did Leo coo?" His eyes searched mine for the answer.

"I don't remember," I said. I looked at David to change my answer, but he just nodded.

"Did you have any concerns about his early development?" he said. "Did he sit, crawl, and walk when you expected?"

"Yes," I said. "He sat up between five and six months and crawled when he was about eight. I remember he was an early walker. Right after he turned one, he started to run."

We revealed everything about Leo's development since birth, but I found it difficult to concentrate. My eyes strayed to Leo moving around the room. The nurse, with a clipboard and pen, scooched over from the back of the couch to get in front of him. She squatted and shoved her face into his, her expression like that of a scary Halloween mask. He ran away, and it took me a moment to process his predicament. Was this a test?

I squirmed and sank deeper into the couch, unsure of what to expect next. The doctor's features turned intense without warning. He latched on to the phrase "sustained social interaction" and manipulated it into a question that seemed more like interrogation. He raised his voice, and his eyes bore into mine. "Can he sustain a social interaction?"

"He plays peekaboo," I said. "For several minutes."

Dr. Sherman didn't break eye contact and drew his brows together. His voice grew louder. "I said, 'Can he sustain a social interaction?'"

I twisted my body. I rubbed my chin to gain time to answer: "No."

He wrote that down and adjourned the interview, leaving to discuss his findings with the nurse.

David and I, looking as disheveled as we felt, were alone with Leo. I thought the evaluation went poorly. Leo was uncooperative but didn't cry. He never looked happy, so his expression was no different from normal. I cradled him, placing his slim white legs over my arms. His skin was cool and dry like paper, and his bright blue eyes met mine.

When Dr. Sherman and the nurse returned, he eased back in his chair with confidence. I could almost catch the word coming out of his mouth: "Ah" . . . "tis". . . ."em."

"Your son is autistic. I'm sure of it." My face crumbled, and my eyes burned with tears. I felt as if I carried the pain of all the parents who had ever been told that their child had a disability, and I knew that my life would be changed forever.

The doctor threw this terrifying word at me without offering a clear understanding of what autism involved and what we were up against. I did not know then that the field had conflicting views and opinions about the disorder, and doctors approached diagnosing and treating it differently.

But the doom that just the word implied was simply something I could not accept. It was difficult at first to distinguish between being motivated by the hope of proving the doctor wrong and the motivation that came from wanting to set Leo on the correct path. I became charged with emotion—first denial and then anger. I was not in denial that Leo had autistic-like characteristics, but I could not believe that he met all of the criteria for autism. I felt angry at myself for thinking that I may have caused Leo's condition by carelessly overlooking some minor precaution during my pregnancy. I felt angry at Leo, which was the hardest feeling to bear.

Then, a week later, our shock and grieving became universal when terrorists attacked the World Trade Center and the Pentagon. We felt that not only had we lost a loved one in Leo, but that the expectations every parent has for the future triumphs of their children were undermined. But most particularly, we ached for Leo. Maybe he wouldn't go to college. Maybe he wouldn't get married. Maybe he would always be dependent on us. Maybe he would suffer always from "extreme social isolation," as the terrifying clinical language put it.

After the evaluation, I did not go back to the routine of family life. I no longer had a routine. I had a mission—to find out what was wrong and get Leo the help he needed. A friend told me about the Yale Child Study Center, one of the top evaluation centers for diagnosing autism spectrum disorders. The waiting list for children over three was two-and-a-half years. When I called and said Leo had just turned two, the intake person booked us an appointment within five months, which was reduced to two months after somebody else canceled their appointment.

The Second Opinion

Three weeks before the Yale evaluation, I filled out a stack of forms, including the MacArthur Communicative Development Inventory: Words and Gestures; the Communication and Symbolic Behavior Scales; and the Infant/Toddler Checklist for Communication and Language Development. The only question I vividly remember asked for an example of symbolic play. I racked my brain but could come up with only one example: Leo had used a triangular-shaped No Smoking sign as a tunnel for one of his trains.

At Yale's request, I also took Leo for other tests, including a

DNA blood test to rule out the presence of fragile X, which is a genetic defect that is linked to autism and is the most common cause of inherited mental retardation in boys. Some of its symptoms—repetitive body movements and poor eye contact—are mistaken for autism. The blood test concluded that Leo did not have fragile X. The second test, called an Audio Brainstem Response Test, which measures brainwave activity in the auditory centers of the brain, could not be administered because Leo wouldn't fall asleep after drinking a sleep medication.

The Yale evaluation room looked like a large walk-in closet, but the walls were bare. A small table and chair were placed in front of the one-way mirror. I observed Leo behind the mirror. David stayed with Leo.

The examiner, Dr. Chawarska, pulled out the Autism Diagnostic Observation Scale–Generic (ADOS–G) testing materials—bags filled with miniature toys and other objects. She used these materials to place Leo in a variety of real-life activities that demanded specific social reactions—smiling, pointing, participating, or offering to share.

Leo walked over to a box on top of a small table. The box was closed, and he wanted Dr. Chawarska to open it. Leo said, "Open," but he didn't direct his voice and eyes at her. I waited for him to place the box in her hands, but he didn't. She opened the box and placed several items on the table—a key, two identical cars, two pieces of yarn, a book, a toy telephone, and a block covered with sandpaper. Leo picked up the key and moved it close to his eyes. He raised the key above his head and observed this new visual angle. He then examined the edges of the table from several different perspectives.

"Look at the cars," said David.

"Please don't say anything," said Dr. Chawarska. She did not want David to redirect him.

The sandpaper-covered block also caught Leo's attention. When he attempted to chew on it, she pulled the block away from his mouth. The intrusion upset Leo. He flapped his hands and momentarily bent his wrists and positioned his cupped hands under his chin.

Dr. Chawarska put away the toys and gave Leo another task—operating a pop-up toy. Leo could not figure out which direction to turn the knobs and levers to activate the lids so that the animal characters popped up. Frustrated, he stepped away from the table and moved about the room, squinting, pacing along the wall, and walking in circles. These activities distressed him, and Dr. Chawarska said he could take a break. David showed him a favorite book we had brought and offered him a snack to calm him down.

Another examiner led me to a windowless office with bright lights and began asking me questions from the Vineland Adaptive Behavior Scales, Expanded Version. The Vineland is a general developmental test that is based on parent observations and widely used to evaluate communication, social, and daily living skills of children.

"Does he turn his eyes and head toward sound?" the examiner said.

"No."

"Does he listen, at least momentarily, when you speak to him?"

"No," I said.

"Does he smile when he sees you?"

"Sometimes."

"Does he raise his arms when you say, 'Come here' or 'Up'?"

"No," I said.

"Does he demonstrate understanding of the meaning of 'no'?" said the examiner.

"No."

"Does he gesture appropriately to indicate 'yes,' 'no,' and 'I want'?"

"No."

I had tried to remember what Lucas did at Leo's age to help me determine whether Leo's behavior was out of the normal range. To a clinician, the normal range is quantified in data that compares the individual test score of one child to the test scores of a large group of same-aged children. For me, it was the source of discomfort and fear. Most of the time, I saw the differences between Lucas and Leo in stereo.

The examiner continued. Could Leo drink from a cup? Could he suck from a straw? Could he feed himself with a fork? Could he brush his teeth without help? Did he indicate a soiled diaper by pointing or vocalizing? No, no, no, all of them no, except for one. Leo sucked strongly from a straw. On Leo's play and social skills, I had to admit he had limited interactions with peers. He didn't play with common household objects. He didn't call me "Mommy" or his dad "Daddy." But I was happy when I could answer yes when she asked if he liked cause-and-effect activities; he loved to stand on a stool and flick the light switch on and off.

The last set of questions focused on eye-hand coordination. Leo disliked puzzles. They were too hard for him, and he could barely throw, much less catch, a ball. I remember Lucas throwing a Nerf ball at him, again and again, and Leo had stood there with his arms plastered to his sides. He didn't naturally react. The ball hit him in the face, and he just winced.

During the evaluation, Leo repeated phrases from familiar books, such as *The Three Billy Goats Gruff*. He said, "Mean and ugly troll!" and "Get out of my way!" He never spoke an original phrase or sentence during the entire exercise. I did not want to believe that Leo had echolalia (*echo-lay-le-ah*) as Dr. Sherman had pointed out in his report. But, in fact, Leo did. Echolalia, a common feature of children on the spectrum, causes a child to repeat things they've heard, either immediately, days, weeks, months, or even years later.

Echolalia disturbed me because it was just plain weird. I imagined psychotic homeless men shouting out at imaginary people. I wanted to extinguish it immediately, but the speech and language pathologist who tested Leo on the second day of the evaluation said echolalia was another positive sign. It showed that Leo's speech was developing.

At the end, David and I met with Drs. Chawarska and Fred Volkmar, the codirector of the center, and the other examiners to discuss the results. Everyone in the room turned toward Dr. Volkmar. He used words economically and in a language I could understand. I listened carefully, absorbing his words diligently, hungrily. He prefaced the diagnosis with a few words, but I only remembered him saying "autism spectrum" and that Leo failed to meet the criteria for pure autism.

He threw in a new diagnosis—the one I had "wanted." While still on the spectrum, a diagnosis of pervasive developmental disorder–not otherwise specified (PDD–NOS), which is often less severe, allowed me to continue to deny and reject the devastating word "autism."

I felt relieved and vindicated, although I held out hope that the doctors would identify some other developmental disorder that would be easier to treat successfully.

The Yale experts recommended the book *More Than Words* by Fern Sussman. It gave me a greater understanding of how I should talk and interact with Leo and explained, in plain English, the terms used by speech therapists. I searched websites to fill gaps in my knowledge about applied behavior analysis (ABA), speech and language pathology, sensory integration, visual-spatial processing, clinical trials, and bilateral coordination.

They also recommended behavior modification, or ABA. Dr. Volkmar told me it could be done without a lot of repetitive and structured table-top activities. Dr. Volkmar had sat on a national panel of federal and autism experts who analyzed ten major intervention models from across the nation. The panel's work culminated in the book *Educating Children with Autism*, which was released the same month Leo turned two. The book recommended no less than twenty-five hours of therapy per week—including both one-on-one instruction in "structured" and "naturalistic environments," and that's what was written into Leo's evaluation report from Yale. Reading thirty-one single-spaced pages on Leo's atypical development and what I should do to intervene was quite a contrast to the couple of paragraphs and check boxes I got from my older son's preschool.

◄ PRACTICAL ADVICE ►

If You Suspect Autism: What to Do

Sometimes parents hesitate to get a diagnosis, either because they don't acknowledge the warning signs or don't want to label their child at such a young age. That's understandable. Many specialists say autism isn't identifiable until a child is at least eighteen months of age, when the behaviors that are its core defining features start to become more apparent.

If your pediatrician or other health care professional suggests that you wait, don't. First, it can take several months to schedule an appointment for an evaluation. Make one. You can always cancel it. Waiting also delays the diagnosis—and the treatment—to an average age of between three and six years. Studies show that the earlier the treatment, the better the prognosis.[5] If you can come at a moment's notice, ask the intake person to put you on the cancellation list, and call back every few weeks to check the status of your appointment. Even in the world of health care, the cranky wheel does get served first.

You have two options in getting an evaluation. You can find a specialist, or take advantage of publicly funded early intervention programs, which support families and treat babies and toddlers until they turn three years old. These programs are run by counties and states and funded through your tax dollars. They were created under federal special education law, known as the Individuals with Disabilities Education Act, commonly referred to as IDEA.

Each route—public and private—has its own set of thorns and roses, and it is important to understand them in deciding which direction is optimal for your child and family needs.

Under federal special education law, your child has the right to be evaluated for special education services and, if found eligible, to receive a free and appropriate public education, known as a FAPE.

The first question: How old is your child?

Answering this will determine which program to call since publicly funded services are generally divided between children under three years old and children three and older.

If Your Child Is Under Three

For children under three, you want to identify a program under your state's early intervention services.

Each state has an early intervention program, but no two program names are alike. Some are called Early On, Together We Grow, Child Find (one of the more common names), Baby Watch, or First Steps. Your goal is to get to your local early intervention office. The National Dissemination Center for Children with Disabilities, which is the official national clearinghouse for providing information on these services, can tell you. You can visit the site's *State Resources* page* to find contact numbers for programs with age ranges associated with them, or just send an email to nichcy@aed.org. The organization answers emails promptly. If all else fails, call its toll-free number, (800) 695-0285, and tell the operator that you want to talk to an information specialist. The District of Columbia number is (202) 884-8200.

* www.nichcy.org/states.htm

It gets even more complicated because revisions to the law in 2004 added "early intervening services (EIS)" for children age three through high school. EIS is not the same thing as early intervention, even though they both are about intervening early. EIS is about catching problems early in school-aged children who are struggling to learn and then intervening to help them. Early intervention, on the other hand, is about identifying developmental delays and disorders in infants and toddlers and working with families to develop an action plan, called an IFSP (Individualized Family Service Plan), to help their child overcome his or her difficulties as much as possible.

Early intervention services are generally free to parents, but some states, such as Ohio, charge for certain specialized services, including family visits and home training. Whether or not you're asked to cover a portion of the cost depends on your income and the rules in your state.

Who Refers Your Child

You can request an evaluation for your child. If your child attends preschool or is in child care, be it public or private, your child's teacher or child-care provider also can make a referral. Of course, you will need to give permission—and make sure it's in writing—before any action is taken.

Once a referral is made, your state sets the rules for when it will conduct an evaluation and deliver services, provided your child is eligible to receive them. Although IDEA specifies a sixty-day time frame for this process, states are allowed to set their own timelines, and that's the one that will apply to you. States cannot, however, exceed what's written into the federal law.

Pay attention to these timelines. If they are not met, it will help support any legal proceeding you bring. Your state education department is one source to find out what timelines apply in your state. Go back to the "State Resources" page of the dissemination center's site,* choose your state, and then scroll down the list of agencies until you find the heading "State Education Department: Special Education." Call the number listed.

At private diagnostic centers, especially the better-known ones, you also might face a long waiting list. Of course, there is nothing you can do but wait—or find another private evaluator. Some centers have waiting lists of more than two years. Private evaluations also are expensive, running into the hundreds, if not thousands, of dollars. Getting your health insurer to pay for an evaluation is another battle.

The law governing special education is wickedly complex, and parents' experience with it ranges from good to bad, since states are allowed to write their own rules to interpret the federal law. State education departments are under tremendous pressure to cut costs, and the law isn't always interpreted to please parents. You have good reason to be skeptical of how your state interprets the law, but that doesn't mean you shouldn't try to take advantage of its intended benefits—and avoid its pitfalls. Evaluations, therapies, and special schools are expensive, and many families lack the resources to bypass the law and pay out of pocket.

Networking with other parents is the best way to scope out the quality of services in your area. If you belong to a church or synagogue or other faith-based group, see if it has a support group for parents of children with special needs. Attend a meeting and ask for their experiences. They'll want to help.

Another starting point is to go online and retrieve your state's federal monitoring report from the U.S. Department of Education's Office of Special Education Programs. These reports—for infants and toddlers,† and school-aged children‡—identify the strengths

* www.nichcy.org/states.htm
† www.ed.gov/fund/data/report/idea/partcvvltr/index.html
‡ www.ed.gov/fund/data/report/idea/partbvvltr/index.html

and weaknesses in your state's programs as well as areas of non-compliance.

In June 2007, the U.S. Department of Education for the first time issued IDEA Report Cards for the fifty states and eight territories.* Only fourteen states met the standards of their infant and toddler programs, while five failed and the rest need assistance. The news was just as sobering for school districts: nine states met the grade; the remaining forty-one states all need help to implement the requirements of federal special education law.

Given the surge in cases, it should come as no surprise if the programs in your state fail to meet obligations under the federal law. In the last decade, the number of children diagnosed with autism and served under IDEA skyrocketed by more than 500 percent, with most states reporting double- and triple-digit increases, according to federal figures.

If Your Child Is Three or Older

A frustrating and confusing problem is getting to the right person to schedule an evaluation if your child is three or older. In this case, it's best to call your neighborhood elementary school and speak to the principal. Explain that you suspect a developmental delay and that you want to get your child evaluated. The principal is likely to put you in touch with the school psychologist or person in charge of overseeing special education services for the school. Sometimes these specialists are shared among schools and won't be in when you call. You'll have to leave a message. And put your emotions aside, as hard as it is. Speak with confidence and act in a businesslike manner. From the school district's perspective, this is business.

---

* www.ed.gov/policy/speced/guid/idea/monitor/factsheet.html

If you can't get ahold of the principal, call your school district office and ask for the chairperson of the Committee on Preschool Special Education. Many principals are either ignorant or not motivated to help and might point you in another direction altogether.

Some principals, however, are proud of the special education services they offer and might put you in touch with a parent whose child is receiving services at the school. Politely take the name but don't rely on this parent's insight alone. Remember, the school wants to present you with a poster parent who represents the school favorably; you want the inside scoop from in-the-know parents. Local support groups are a prime source of information.

Another important point is that the diagnostic methods used by schools will be different from those used by private evaluators. Schools want to prepare your child for academic success—cutting paper, writing, reading—while you might be more interested in teaching your child how to make friends or button a shirt. Disagreements over goals often lead to conflicts that cannot always be resolved without a court fight.

Your child also might not receive a diagnosis as a result of a school evaluation but still qualify for special education services by meeting specific eligibility criteria based on a particular diagnosis, or being classified as "developmentally delayed." Schools have some leeway about how they handle the labeling process. Moreover, schools are not obligated to accept the results from a private evaluation, but many do because it saves them the cost of performing their own.

Getting a Private Evaluation

If you choose a private evaluation, ask your pediatrician to recommend a team of professionals who has extensive experience evaluating autism spectrum disorders. Autism is too complex—and serious—a disorder for one person to diagnose accurately, especially in children who are mildly affected. This "multidisciplinary team" is jargon for a group of professionals representing a cross section of medical, communication, and behavior specialties.

Generally, you'll want either a developmental pediatrician, pediatric neurologist, child psychiatrist or psychologist, and a certified speech-language pathologist, behavior therapist, and/or physical or occupational therapist. How you portray your concerns and answer questions on intake forms will drive who's involved on your team. If you want to explore medication, for example, expect a specialist, such as a pediatric psychopharmacologist, to be included.

Is Your Head in the Sand?

The diagnosis of autism incapacitates many parents, even though they understand the logic that early detection and treatment improve outcomes. But the power of denial is incredibly strong, and it has nothing to do with your education, wealth, ethnicity, or race. It is not unheard of for well-educated and financially secure families to divert their attention from helping their child to renovating their house because they don't want to face the pain of confronting their child's challenges. Of course, it's easier to scrutinize paint chips than to face the possibility that your child might acquire only a few words over the course of his life. Sadly, between 35 percent and 40 percent of children diagnosed with a spectrum disorder, at least at present, won't develop functional speech, but this number is decreasing over time with earlier diagnosis. Some children, however, are highly verbal.

In the past, perhaps 75 percent of children with classical autism also had mental retardation, but with intervention and earlier diagnosis, this number seems to be decreasing. Mental retardation is uncommon in children with Asperger's disorder.

Top Diagnostic Centers

These centers will evaluate children under eighteen months old but won't always give a firm diagnosis. Since the cause of autism is unknown, which means there are no medical tests, the diagnosis is based on observing a child's communication, behavior, and developmental levels.

▶ **Albert Einstein College of Medicine of Yeshiva University**
CHILDREN'S EVALUATION AND REHABILITATION CENTER
The RELATE (Rehabilitation, Evaluation, and Learning for Autistic Infants and Toddlers at Einstein) Program
Bronx, New York
(718) 430-3914
www.aecom.yu.edu/cerc/relate.htm
Uses the "gold standard" of diagnostic tests, known as the Autism Diagnostic Observation Schedule, or ADOS. The center has offered "provisional" diagnoses to children as young as one year.

▶ **Kennedy Krieger Institute's Center for Autism and Related Disorders**
Baltimore, Maryland
(443) 923-9200
(800) 873-3377
www.kennedykrieger.org
Kennedy will evaluate children and identify those "at risk" for an autism spectrum disorder but won't diagnose children under eighteen months. You can obtain an online appointment request form at www.kennedykrieger.org/kki_online_appt.jsp.

▶ **The LADDERS Clinic**
Wellesley, Massachusetts
(781) 449-6074
www.ladders.org

LADDERS has diagnosed a child as young as twelve months of age. The diagnostic test varies, depending on physician. Some physicians use ADOS.

▶ **University of Washington Autism Center**
Seattle, Washington
(206) 221-6806
http://depts.washington.edu/uwautism
While it shies away from formal diagnosis for one-year-olds, the center evaluates the child's behaviors and follows up at eighteen months.

▶ **Yale Child Study Center**
New Haven, Connecticut
(203) 785-2874 or (203) 785-3488
http://info.med.yale.edu/chldstdy
The center will provide a provisional diagnosis for babies and toddlers and annual follow-up until age four. After that, children age out of the "baby clinic" and are placed on the waiting list of several years. The center uses the Autism Diagnostic Observation Schedule, or ADOS.

What to Expect During an Evaluation or Assessment

Having your child evaluated for an autism spectrum disorder is one of the most traumatic experiences you'll ever face. If your suspicions are confirmed, the word that people have been whispering under their breath will sound like a shout in your ears.

Your hopes will be dashed, and you'll cry—a lot. This is not what parenthood is supposed to be about.

In addition, an evaluation, whether private or through early intervention services, will be exhausting for you and your child. Some evaluations last two half-days, and that doesn't include tests you might be asked to complete in advance of your appointment. These tests are generally meant to rule out other conditions, such as whether your child has a hearing loss, possesses a genetic defect, or is prone to seizures.

Prep Work

The intake person who schedules your appointment will guide you through the process of what, if any, tests your child needs before you come. You'll also get forms to sign and fill out and a list of records to assemble. Some forms about your child's development ask you to write your concerns, darken circles (as in an SAT test), or circle a number based on a scale. It's okay to circle two numbers and draw an arrow between them if you believe your child falls somewhere in the middle. Just be honest with your answers and try to make copies of the filled-out forms before you send them back in.

You should also:

▸ Ask for the names of the professionals who will be evaluating your child. You want a team evaluation because there isn't one professional who will be able to evaluate the spectrum of deficits, from social skills to language to sensory issues, in your child.

▸ Ask for the names of the diagnostic tools they will use. Use the Internet to understand more about these tests. Familiarizing yourself with them will help ease your anxiety. Your intake coordinator also can help answer more in-depth questions. Don't worry if you find the information difficult to understand. The learning curve is steep.

▸ Maintain your child's daily routine and offer healthy foods. You can only do so much to prepare your child. You can't train your child to behave or play with toys appropriately.

▸ When traveling, eating right is often difficult. Make sure you pack a variety of snacks you know your child loves.

▸ Help your child understand that he will be playing with many different people and that either his mommy or his daddy will stay in the room with him. Even if you think your child lacks the capacity to understand, the emotional reassurance you offer might register.

▸ Ask if you will be assigned a social worker to follow up with once the evaluation is over and you're back home.

Evaluation Day

Don't go alone. Bring your spouse or friend. You'll need the support of someone to see you through this experience. Your child also needs a familiar caregiver to stay with him when you're called away to answer questions about your child's development and family dynamics. You don't want to leave your child with a stranger during these interview sessions, and you shouldn't be asked to do so. You also don't want to answer questions with your child crawling or running around the room; it's too distracting for everyone involved.

Your observations and concerns should be taken seriously and are but one piece of the puzzle to determine what may be wrong. During the evaluation, an examiner will present your child with a set of tasks involving toys, objects, puzzles, blocks, or other items, or may seek to engage your child in a social activity, such as a mock birthday party. How your child reacts is yet another piece of the puzzle. Depending on your child's age, he or she may be given an

IQ test. Other likely tests will measure your child's language and communication skills against what would be expected of same-aged typically developing children.

If your child's behavior surprises you, say so. Another question examiners ask is whether your child's performance represents behavior that's typical for your child. Just be honest.

Other important points:

▸ Bring along some of your child's favorite toys or a comfort item to help him relax.

▸ Ask to take a break if your child becomes too frustrated or agitated during an evaluation activity.

▸ Don't be afraid to challenge the examiner. You are the expert when it comes to your child.

▸ Have a favorite video ready to play for your feedback session. After the evaluation, the specialists should either give you a diagnosis or their impressions about your concerns. You'll get about twenty minutes of their time, and you don't want your child distracting you as you take notes. This is your opportunity to nail down some specific recommendations for intervention before you receive your written report, which could take several weeks to complete. Take it.

▸ **FAST FACT**

A comprehensive private evaluation can cost from $500 to $5,000. Add in the cost of therapies: occupational and speech-language ($90 an hour to more than $100 an hour); special ed schools (upwards of $30,000 a year); and weekly visits to other specialists, such as child psychologists and behavioral pediatricians ($100 an hour to more than $200 an hour), and the financial burden of raising a child with autism comes into much sharper focus.

▷ Don't ask the specialists to give you a prognosis. They can't. What they can do is tell you if there are any positive prognostic signs.

Should You Get a Second Opinion?

Don't shop for a diagnosis. However, you may have valid reasons to pursue a second opinion. A second opinion will help reassure you that the diagnosis is either valid or incorrect. Remember, autism spectrum disorders are diagnosed based on symptoms, which are largely behavioral, as opposed to its cause, which we don't really know. This leaves room to subjectively interpret the behavioral descriptions found in diagnostic tools.

If you question the diagnosis but aren't in denial that something is wrong, a prudent approach is to develop an intervention plan to start treatment while you are looking for a second opinion. While a correct diagnosis helps guide the particulars in an intervention plan, if your child cannot talk, your child is going to need speech therapy. You can always adjust and make your child's intervention plan more comprehensive as you learn more. There is more upside than downside in this approach, and no time will be lost.

FOUR

▶ ▶ ▶ ▶ # Coping with a Diagnosis: What You and Your Family Are In For

After Leo's diagnosis, the hardest thing was trying to live like a normal family. The diagnosis had changed our lives profoundly. It was difficult to engage in social activities with the boys when we were around parents with typical children. Either David or I would need to be on "Leo duty" to keep him from exploring—a polite way of saying "wandering off."

When our older son, Lucas, received a birthday invitation from one of his classmates in September 2001, I decided to take Leo, now twenty-seven months, to the party while David stayed home. I was as eager to go as Lucas was. I longed to chitchat with other adults, and Lucas, naturally outgoing and gregarious, was in the early stages of discovering what parties were all about.

Leo, on the other hand, did not comprehend the meaning of party, and I didn't prepare him for the event. I didn't think he'd understand or that it would make a difference if I told him what to expect. I often carted him around like a handbag so I could get my errands done. I knew that I could have told him we were flying to the moon and he would have had the same reaction as if I had said we were going to the grocery store.

The challenge Leo faced in social situations had not yet become evident to me. I didn't think ahead about how Leo would react when placed in the company of ten boisterous boys who were two years older than him. Taking him was not a test to see how well he'd do in the company of other children—just a case of clueless-ness on my part.

When we arrived, the front door was unlocked, so we walked into the foyer. Karen, the mother, came to greet us. She looked younger than me, a plus-sized woman with her hair worn in wispy black curls, and her lips and nails painted vibrant pink. Karen looked at me, then Leo and Lucas, and then back at me. She took the present I handed her while I blurted out, "Leo is autistic."

There was an awkward moment of silence and a stunned expression on Karen's face before she adjusted to crack a small smile. "Well, I'm glad you came," she said, her voice tightening. "Let me show you the playroom."

Looking back, I confessed to Karen because I wanted her to be extra kind to me, as people do when a loved one dies and they crave sympathy. It had only been two weeks since Leo's diagnosis, and I couldn't think about much else. I had suffered an enormous loss that was very, very real and was in shock, still grieving and adjusting. The birthday party created another episode of fresh grief because it reminded me that Leo would not celebrate his fourth birthday surrounded by young friends. Again, I felt that crushing loss of hope.

Karen led us to the playroom. I now realized the obvious—that I should have left Leo at home with his father. Leo squirmed and broke loose from my arms. All of the other children ignored him. I can't blame them. They didn't know Leo. They were a bunch of four-year-olds whose own social skills were pretty rudimentary. I couldn't stand to see Leo ignored, so I started playing with him the best I could. There were heaps of Fisher-Price toys strewn around the room. Leo showed little interest in them and constantly headed for the open door that led to the kitchen. I felt uneasy and trapped and couldn't wait for the party to be over.

The time I spent in the playroom felt like an eternity when it was probably no more than forty-five minutes. Karen didn't check on me. No one did. When it came time for lunch, Karen opened the door to the playroom and called the children. I told Lucas to go and eat.

Alone in the playroom, I worked to play with Leo. And it *was* work—to get his attention, and to hold his attention. I blocked him from running upstairs, but he got away and I had to retrieve him before he made it to the top of the stairs.

Coming down the stairs, I looked into the mirror overhanging the fireplace mantel and saw the reflection of Karen removing the last dirty plate from the table. I thought now would be a good time to make an appearance. If there was one thing about Leo, he loved cake, especially chocolate. When Leo and I entered the room, Karen was lighting the candles, and everyone waited for her cue to sing "Happy Birthday." We rushed to sit down on the placeholder chair that remained as all eyes shifted to Kevin. After an off-key rendition of the song, Kevin made a wish, and the table erupted in cheers and applause when he blew out all his candles. As Karen was passing out the cake, she groped for words to ask if Leo would like a piece. Flustered, she stopped in mid-sentence and finally placed one piece of cake in front of us. I sensed that her brief observation of Leo had led her to believe that because he couldn't talk or interact, he wouldn't notice, or care, if he didn't get his own piece of cake. Without asking if we'd like another fork, Karen moved on to the next person.

I was too stunned to assert myself and ask for another one. Leo and I alternated eating bits of cake sharing the one fork. I sensed his pleasure as he relaxed against me and ate the sweet icing. I rubbed my tears before they became evident and felt as though I had died.

After we finished our cake, we left in a hurry. I forced myself to thank Karen for inviting us and strode, head down, seething, enraged, out the front door. My entire body shook, and I did not look back.

Being treated like an outcast was unprecedented for me and struck a nerve that I did not know existed. I did not understand how Karen could have been so cruel. I wanted her to have a child with special needs so she could feel what it was like. But also I'd been raised with my parents' usual prejudices against people who were disabled, who make us normal people feel uncomfortable because they are weird, incomplete, maybe even contagious. And now, by some Karmic accident, I'd been grouped with the abnormal. The idea that from this point forward the world would see me for my wounds and not my bravery left me in despair.

I never brought up the incident with Karen since we were not friends, and I didn't know what to say. Although forgiving is central to my Christian faith, I have not entirely forgiven her, and I cannot forget. For years I carried deep, unresolved feelings about the party, and, these feelings would rise again with every birthday invitation Lucas received and then again when Leo entered preschool and started receiving invitations. Birthdays, for me, no longer meant carrot cake at the cherry dining room table in the house where I grew up.

Instead, I felt what rehabilitation counselor Simon Olshanksy termed "chronic sorrow," meaning a continuous grieving process that persists. Somewhere out there, perhaps—after we found a new house in a new city, found schools and services, after Leo began to show signs of overcoming some of his challenges, after I got back on a regular exercise schedule and we were surrounded by a tight-knit social network, after a good long string of accomplishments—joy might return. But it seemed to me on that day of the party that triumph was a very long way off.

Leo's Residual Issues

The worst days were not always the earliest ones. Even after Leo lost his diagnosis, residual issues persisted. Leo was both fragile and unstable—and unpredictable in the way he dealt with his emotions, keeping me in a perpetual loop of angst, constantly worrying that he'd blow up at something other children might furrow their brows at. I felt as if other parents constantly passed judgment on me and my son when he acted out.

His emotions were bound by chaos and rigidity, and he had trouble finding emotional harmony. Sometimes, he'd cry if he couldn't find his seamless socks, or he'd lash out, saying, "Have fun being the worst mom ever," when I'd play with Lucas instead of him. His behavior often spilled over to school and in public places. If the chocolate shake machine at the diner was broken, he'd burst into tears, refusing the next best substitute, chocolate milk. At school, he'd speak what would be my hidden thoughts. During a field trip, he yelled, "I hate science." My eyes blazed with embarrassment.

Even years after the birthday party incident, I cringed every time I had to wait in the pickup line at preschool and make small talk. What did the moms think of me and my son? I imagined it went like this: "He cries all the time. What's wrong with him? We won't ask him over for a playdate." Leo is my son. I love him, and I'm desperate to help him work through his frustration. If you only knew what we've been through. You'll see. I'll show you. Leo will show you. He may have a testy temperament, but he's an exceptionally bright child, maybe even a genius, and I'm going to get him out of this school and find a classroom of children that will revel in his colorful use of language and appreciate his bravado. He won't be like this when he's sixteen. He can't be like this. I'm counting on him learning how to work through his frustration—for my sake. I need a life, too.

◄ **PRACTICAL ADVICE** ►

After the blow of the diagnosis, you'll move through the seven stages of grief, which psychiatrist Elisabeth Kübler-Ross describes as shock or disbelief, denial, bargaining, guilt, anger, depression, and acceptance and hope. Your journey through these stages will occur at your own pace and in your own way, often without a defining line between each stage.

As you cope with an emotional stew of feelings—frustration, exhaustion, anxiety, rejection, stress, and possibly depression— your natural defense mechanism to "compartmentalize" your thoughts might kick in. Compartmentalizing is a psychological term that means to separate different aspects of your life into baskets in order to focus on a task. For example, you need to separate your thoughts from your daily tasks. Spend a half hour making telephone calls, the next hour filling out forms, and another block of time doing something else. It boils down to focus and not letting your emotions intrude on what you're doing. Planning your day like this sounds rigid, but you'll accomplish more. If your child is newly diagnosed, your first task is finding a team of trusted experts who can help you weigh the pros and cons about educational and treatment programs in *your* area.

Finding the right team will help you feel more empowered and relieve some of the stress. But securing that team is stressful, as you'll be taking several actions simultaneously—calling experts, running into bureaucratic policies, conducting research, taking notes, keeping records, visiting programs, fighting with your health insurer and/or school district, making decisions, and balancing the needs of other family members.

You might feel, as I did, that you're being evicted from a life that suddenly bucked you off into a new and unknown world.

In coping with my son's diagnosis and treatment, I tried to follow the advice of Leo's psychologist. On every visit, she encouraged me to make time for myself and not feel guilty. I followed this advice, leaning more heavily on the things I always did to relieve stress: I ran or watched television or got that manicure or I drank wine with dinner. I didn't use any of these activities to avoid helping my child, such as taking up long-distance running, adopting a TV addiction, or drinking a whole bottle of wine at a time. I found it difficult, however, to make time for other family members, especially my older son, who felt confused and frustrated because I paid so much attention to Leo. Doing something special with him, such as taking him to a movie or to Payless for new shoes, was something that I wished I had more energy for.

My husband and I didn't see a marriage counselor, though I could have used guidance to help me communicate better and even argue in a healthier way. But in the end, when we needed the most help, we couldn't afford it, and there never seemed to be enough time to schedule yet another appointment. As it was, we settled for

▶ **INFORM YOURSELF** ─────────────────────────────

Five Tips for Coping

How often do you find yourself saying, "How am I going to cope? I'm physically exhausted and emotionally drained."

Find a skillful and trusted team of professionals. Assemble a group that is dedicated to helping you and your child. They are likely to include therapists, a psychologist or psychiatrist (or both), teachers, social workers, or a developmental pediatrician. The makeup of your team depends on your child's needs.

Take a break. You'll need one, because you're running a marathon, not a sprint. You'll also run out of patience and need the time to regain your

continues on next page . . .

emotional balance. Enlist the help of your spouse to take care of your child while you enjoy a favorite activity. Follow your lead on what rejuvenates you, and try not to feel guilty. If you don't make time for yourself, you'll burn out.

Get informed. Knowledge, as Sir Francis Bacon wrote in the sixteenth century, is power, so learn as much as you can about the disorder. There are myths and misconceptions about autism. Rely on your team for advice about treatments and educational programs. Don't be misled by what you read online or what other parents tell you about alternative treatments. Protect your financial resources.

Network with other families. Talking it out with other families is a good stress buster. Locate support groups through your church, synagogue, or other faith-based group. Also, check your public elementary school and early intervention office to see if there's a parent support group. Many times members have dealt with cutting through red tape or navigating the school system. Their advice will give you direction and confidence. Other places to find support are local chapters of Families for Early Autism Treatment,[*] the Autism Society of America[†] and Parents of Autistic Children.[‡] There also are numerous email discussion lists. You can find them at Yahoo! Groups,[§] Google Groups[**] and Topica.[††]

Eat healthy and exercise. Regular exercise improves your body's ability to reduce stress and helps clear your mind. You don't need to vigorously jump rope to reduce stress. Something simple and safe, such as stretching and walking, will also release tension. Sleep also provides relaxation and rest. Drink as much water as possible and try to include more whole and fewer processed foods, though there's nothing wrong with a pizza on a Friday night when you're ready to collapse.

[*] www.feat.org
[†] www.autism-society.org
[‡] www.poac.net
[§] http://groups.yahoo.com
[**] http://groups.google.com
[††] http://lists.topica.com

going out when we could find a babysitter, which posed its own set of challenges.

Finally, guiding my son through a childhood strewn with obstacles could have effectively destroyed my marriage. Try as I might, I was inattentive to Lucas and David and, upon occasion, essentially absent. (My bedtime got progressively earlier as I wearily collapsed after stressful days.)

I spent my days managing Leo's therapy, which included rounding up student therapists, who often quit on me without warning; scouting for programs that embraced inclusion and Floortime; ramping up the number of hours Leo spent in therapy—from eight hours a week up to more than twenty-five; finding schools; looking for psychologists trained in applied verbal behavior (AVB); and driving all over the place to take Leo to occupational therapy, speech therapy, or some social skills group. During Leo's longer therapy sessions, I scurried to Frederick, Maryland, to review video tapes of him to enhance my instruction of AVB or consulted with my lawyer and educational advocate over the bungling of special education services offered by the District of Columbia. I cried more than once under the pressure.

Everyone recognized my preoccupation was for a good cause, but people can bend only so far before they break. I tried very consciously not to become the CEO of the Leo Project and make significant decisions independent of David's input. My husband always asked the difficult questions about a potential therapy before it could become part of Leo's regime, but he never said no. While his engagement was less than mine, I found that explaining our next decision helped me to understand it better. And David's critical thinking skills were vital on more than one occasion.

Experts say that the central family dynamics are reordered in all families confronting the illness of a child, whatever the diagnosis. His or her care becomes the axis around which most everything else revolves—shopping, meals, weekends, schools, vacations, and the rest of the details of daily living. If your "damaged" child is high functioning, he or she soon learns how to manipulate the situation to get more good things and to avoid most bad things. Even if your other children start out sympathetic, there is a time invariably when their goodwill runs out and they resent all the "yeses" their sibling gets at times when they get "nos." This phenomenon also needs to be addressed early, as early as you can see it developing.

It is useless to be told to be fair to your children in their conflicts with one another. Of course you try to be fair. However, when one child is getting most of your time and attention, when you have restructured your life to be that child's full-time assistant, and when you react to the child's tantrums with soothing rather than discipline, your other children are bound to be jealous. There are no instructions I can give on how to handle this except to say you need to know this is coming, prepare for this early, and expect it to be with

▶ **INFORM YOURSELF** ————————————————————————

Having a child with special needs means an enormous investment of time and energy for parents, so much so that siblings often get pushed to the side. Parents often unknowingly force siblings into becoming "little adults," expecting more of them because they can do more, not only for themselves but for others. It is not uncommon for siblings to feel complex emotions—anger, resentment, guilt, embarrassment—and act our their feelings as they learn to accept their special-needs brother or sister. While some show compassion and maturity beyond their years, others perceive they're loved less.

Dr. Vicki Panaccione, founder of the Better Parenting Institute,* offers these recommendations:

▶ Acknowledge your nondisabled child's feelings and support him with empathy. Be careful not to react with horror or anger or be dismissive.

* www.askdrvicki.com

- Reassure your child that she can't "catch it" or didn't do anything to cause it. If there is a genetic link, discuss this only when your child is old enough to understand.
- Reassure your child that someone will take care of him if you need to be out of town for an evaluation with his sibling.
- Spend one-on-one time with the nondisabled child, giving plenty of appropriate attention. If your child feels pushed to the side, medical or behavioral symptoms may emerge.
- Allow your child to participate as much, or as little, in the care of the sibling. Just because your child is healthy and capable does not mean she should have "to do" for her sibling.
- Keep your expectations realistic and allow your child to act his age. There is a tendency to expect more of the nondisabled child or to let him fend for himself.
- Find activities or games both children can do together. Just sitting together watching a movie or cartoons can be a bonding experience.

One well-respected program that helps children cope and air annoyances is Sibshops.* The Sibshops program brings play and discussion groups to more than 200 locations nationwide. Children get to meet other children in similar circumstances and discuss feelings with professionals that they are having difficulty expressing with their parents. Search the Sibshops website to find a Sibshop in your area.

Learn more: Siblings of Children with Autism: A Guide for Families, by Dr. Sandra L. Harris, is a frequently recommended book. Dr. Harris offers advice on how to explain the disorder to children of various ages. For example, take a typically developing two-year-old who sees his disabled sibling acting out of control. Dr. Harris says a child this young might be afraid of his sibling's behavior. Explaining the behavior won't do any good because a child this young does not have the cognitive ability to understand. Instead, offer comfort and reassurance. If the typical child is four years old and asks questions about why his brother can't talk, you can say he hasn't learned how. As your typical child matures, Dr. Harris suggests creating a book about his sibling's autism.

* www.siblingsupport.org

you for as long as your child is in therapy. But if there is one piece of advice I can press upon you, it is to make a special date on a regular basis with your typically developing child—take him to his favorite diner, buy him a treat, hug him, but most of all talk to him and try to get him to explore his feelings with you. Your child who does not suffer from language delays or poor social skills needs intervention, too.

Losing Friends

After Leo's diagnosis, I was more or less blind to the fact that my social network steadily disintegrated. My neighbor had a son about Leo's age who was developing normally. While I appreciated her company, I bristled at anything that could be considered a comparison between her son and mine. We saw less of one another. The same thing was true, more or less, with other parents of young children who were friends and neighbors. My already small network of friends entirely transformed itself as I became close to other women with children in treatment. Some friends deserted me, and others passed judgment and made hurtful comments. I understand that they just didn't know what to say, and there wasn't much I could say in return. I could educate them on the disorder or ignore the comment

▶ **FAST FACT**

The National Autism Association recently launched a telephone counseling service that allows couples to arrange a call with a trained therapist for between $1.19 and $1.57 a minute. The nonprofit's Family First Program* also offers grants of up to $1,000 to help couples pay for the service. You can download a grant application from the association's website.

* www.nationalautismassociation.org/familyfirst2.php

and move on. You can't rehearse how you're going to feel at a given moment; the actual experience will dictate the response you give.

My one-on-one friends and therapists became my support group. As I spent more and more time in the company of mothers with children in therapy, they became my friends and the moms I would set up playdates with. Most of the time, their children faced challenges far more overwhelming than mine. The mothers were adjusting to children with lifelong disabilities and who in some dimensions were never going to grow up. This should have terrified me since it was precisely my worst fear. However, I had confidence that Leo had only a few years of therapy before we could stop, and it reassured me that he was closer to normal than those other kids, which allowed me to cope. I am not proud of this, but that's how it was.

You may find comfort by attending a support group for parents and siblings of children with autism, which is what I did in the beginning until I developed my own network of friends. I never got involved in an online support group but can see how this would be useful, especially if you live in a remote area. Whether you attend a support group or call another parent, I think the interaction with other parents is exceptionally important.

I also sought and received constant reassurance from all of Leo's caregivers that I was doing the right thing. After Leo's therapies, I'd block the door so they'd have to tell me something hopeful before we left. Just a few positive comments about Leo helped me heal.

Sometimes, professional help was diverted from treating him to treating me. In particular, I used as much of Leo's time with a psychologist to get her to listen to me and my problems and, above all, to reassure me that I was doing the right thing and he was getting better. Some sessions were devoted to helping me improve my play skills, recognize Leo's play themes and feelings and help Leo think logically, play symbolically with another child, and deal with his fears when he conjured up scenes that involved good versus evil. We also talked about Leo's relationship with his brother and father. In retrospect, maybe I should have gotten my own therapist, but no one knew me or my child as well.

I also never tried medication to control anxiety or help me sleep, but it might be right for you.

Other than a few short visits alone to my parents to wind down and gain some perspective, I never took an extended vacation from my case management duties, but that may well be a good thing to do.

I didn't have an affair, buy expensive items, engage in big home improvement projects, get my mother to move in to help out, get pregnant to give Leo a younger sibling, adjust the household's diet to exclude foods that some parents said would improve the symptoms of autism, sell my house and use the proceeds for Leo's therapy, or a dozen other things that might have happened. To me all those things were bad ideas, but you may find yourself pursuing one or more out of fear, discomfort, frustration, or necessity.

The right way for you to cope is unique to you. Whatever ways you have of managing your own mental health will be as important to your child's course of treatment as anything else you'll do to help him or her.

FIVE

▶ ▶ ▶ Understanding Autism: A Spectrum of Clues

When Leo was diagnosed, my mind catalogued all the possible causes. Varnishing the wood molding in our home when I was pregnant with Leo stood out as the big one. Had I cut off his oxygen supply while his brain was still forming, causing neurological damage? Did it happen because my obstetrician gave me oxygen during the course of my labor when Leo's fetal heart rate had slowed? Did the choroid plexus cysts my ob-gyn detected during a routine sonogram at seventeen weeks damage his brain? She said they had disappeared at twenty-four weeks. I couldn't imagine it was that one glass of wine I drank to celebrate our third wedding anniversary a week before my due date. I didn't believe a well-educated relative who told me the lard used to fry fast-food chicken nuggets caused Leo's brain to form fewer neural pathways. My reaction echoed the outdated belief that I was at fault for being an inattentive mother.

The Yale experts dismissed the thought that I was to blame.

One of the most disturbing conversations I'd had was with a mother of a boy with autism. A neighbor had suggested I call this mother, whom I had never met. In a phone call, the mother told me that her son would never look her in the eye for more than a flicker of an instant, and there was nothing anyone could do. She told me poor eye contact was the result of autistic children having a shorter than normal brainstem. The brainstem, one of the most primitive structures of the brain, the part that keeps us alive, is attached to the spinal chord at the base of the neck to create the central nervous system. It acts as a relay station that passes messages on to various parts of the body which control functions—heart rate, swallowing, breathing, digestion, urination—that are essential for survival. In humans, it allows for advanced mental thought.

As she spoke, I could sense the bitterness rising in her voice. My stomach tightened until my body caved, leaving me feeling empty and hopeless. I did not want to believe that Leo's poor eye contact would never improve beyond intermittent glances, so I maneuvered the conversation to a close. I felt the same way when another mother told me that her son's "autism comes out when he gets tired." I did not want to believe that I would ever describe Leo this way.

It wasn't until much later that I began to look at other structures of the brain impaired by autism. Although the cause of autism is elusive, autopsies of autistic brains show damage or abnormalities in other areas, particularly the amygdala, which is part of the limbic system, the center of all emotions and from which emerges, for example, the feelings in females to nurse and protect their toddlers or that induce the emotions of fright, passion, love, hate, joy, and sadness. Damage to this area, according to experts, impairs the ability of an individual with autism to recognize social emotions and the meaning of complex facial expressions. And that is one of the things that made autism so horrifying—the thought that Leo would not experience emotions in the way I did as a child and do today. I thought of my childhood memories of when my dad cheered me on to reel in an amberjack, a powerful fighting fish, while we were deep-sea fishing off the Florida coast, or when Mom baked me pecan ball cookies for Christmas. I could not imagine what it would be like if the encouragement Dad gave me was impossible to feel, or if I didn't recognize the love my mother felt for me when she baked my favorite cookies. I did not know whether or not Leo could feel these emotions or others.

Before this, I never had reason to examine my brain. Autism gave me a reason.

◄ PRACTICAL ADVICE ►

Separating Fact from Fiction

It's all in the genes, or is it?

Scientists yearn to know the root causes of autism, as do parents, in order to allow practitioners to diagnose autism earlier, perhaps even at birth through a simple blood test, and maybe even to offer a chance to prevent new cases from forming.

To date, about 10 percent of all children with autism have a recognized genetic disorder. The other 90 percent may have undiscovered mutations of their genes that either cause the disorder or lead to an underlying susceptibility to developing autism if other causative factors are present. Thus, one thrust of current research is to identify the genes that lead to autism, or "autisms," a name so given because many experts believe that autism consists of several disorders. Scientists suspect twenty to one hundred genes may be involved.

Every year, public and private groups spend millions of dollars to identify the causes of autism, and every year there seems to be a new research effort created. These efforts are vital and driven by the steep rise in the rate at which children are diagnosed, now estimated at one child of every one hundred fifty. The prevalence of autism in New Jersey is one child out of every ninety-four—the highest in the nation.

While about 90 percent of autism research has focused on

genetics, emerging knowledge from modern brain science is inform-
ing a better understanding of the "underlying processes," or the
mechanisms by which the brain processes information. While autism
spectrum disorders have long been recognized as a biological and
neurological disorder, neuroscientists are now discovering more
about how the brain works and the impact emotions and experience
have on it. For example, a hot topic among neuroscientists is
whether people with autism have broken "mirror neurons." Mirror
neurons are a set of brain cells found on either side of the head that
are thought to give humans the ability to imagine what it would be
like to be another person when they see that person engaged in an
activity, such as yelling at a rude driver. That's because mirror neurons "mirror," or simulate, the action or intentions and emotions of
others and imprint them in our minds, allowing us to feel their emotional significance. The theory may explain why people cry at sad
movies and get so worked up at sporting events.

Neuroscientists believe that mirror neuron activation is related
to learning, empathy, and imitation. If the mirror neurons of
people with autism are broken, it may provide clues that explain
their inability to interact appropriately with others. While they can
learn to identify an emotional expression—a sad or surprised
look—they may not naturally match it to their own understanding
of what it means to be sad or surprised.

Scientists have also found evidence that autism involves more
regions of the brain than defined in the standard "diagnostic triad,"

▶ **FAST FACT**

Fighting Autism* offers an interactive tool that graphs U.S. autism disability data, rates, statistics, incidence, and prevalence in each state and
U.S. territory. The site's autism maps show autism "hot spots" in school
districts in Pennsylvania.

* www.fightingautism.org/idea/index.php

which identifies deficits in the areas of social interaction, communication, and behavior. The other regions that may be involved control complex visual processing, movement, and "sensory perception," or how the brain interprets incoming information from the five senses. The findings provide additional support for a complex information-processing model for autism—meaning that different parts of the brain have difficulty working together to achieve complex tasks. In other words, autism affects the brain globally.

Another growing area of research is how environmental factors influence brain functioning. "Environmental research will be a much bigger field going forward," said Dr. Thomas Insel, director of the National Institute of Mental Health (NIMH). Dr. Insel said there is a concern among parents that NIMH is focusing too much on genetics and not enough on potential environmental causes, such as the mercury once found in the measels–mumps–rubella (MMR) vaccine and other types of heavy metals.

Although studies disprove the theory that mercury in vaccines could induce autism in children, there are parents who reject assurances that there is no casual link. Many of these parents still blame trace amounts of thimerosal, a mercury preservative in the MMR vaccine that is given to infants between twelve and fifteen months, for triggering autism in their child. The U.S. government phased out thimerosal in the MMR vaccine by 2002.

Some researchers finger environmental toxins as potentially contributing to the dramatic rise in autism diagnoses over the past decade. Just look, they say, at the number of chemicals—up to 100,000—registered for commercial use with the U.S. Environmental Protection Agency. Determining which environmental toxins, if any, play a definitive role in causing autism, however, is unanswered. PCBs (polychlorinated biphenyls), a now-banned cooling agent for large electrical equipment, remain a focus of study, as do pesticides, particularly bug killers that belong to a highly toxic class of insecticides known as organophosphates. The chemicals in this class disrupt the brains and nervous systems in bugs, leading to their eventual death. Another newer class of pesticides that act on the central nervous system of bugs is neonicotinoid, often blamed for the declining population of honeybees. Both of these insecticides are toxic to humans.

Critical changes happen to the brain before birth and in the first five years of life, and young brains that are exposed to toxins can alter the way nerve cells communicate with one other, resulting in long-term neurological damage. Many researchers dismiss that the environment is the culprit. They argue, quite convincingly, that genes play the biggest role. They point to studies that examine the genes of identical twins with autism. Studying identical twins is the classic way for researchers to determine whether a disorder is genetically based. That's because identical twins arise from a single fertilized egg and share the same genes, which makes them more likely to share genetically inherited conditions, such as mental retardation. In fact, if one twin has autism, the other has a 90 percent chance of having some autistic characteristics and a 60 percent risk of having all aspects of the disorder.

Genes are tiny sets of body chemicals that determine how we look and how our bodies grow and develop. Each of our body cells contains about 20,000 to 25,000 genes, which make up larger structures known as chromosomes. Chromosomes come in pairs, just like genes. Humans have twenty-three pairs of chromosomes for a total of forty-six. Half of each pair comes from the mother and the other half is inherited from the father.

The Autism Genome Project, the largest study ever of the disorder, released findings in February 2007 and identified two chromosomal regions or genetic "hot spots"—an unidentified region on chromosome 11, which researchers suspect contain genes associated with autism. The other region associated with the disorder is the deletion in part of a gene known as neurexin 1, one of a family of genes thought to play an important role in nerve cell communication. Autism is also associated with a defect on chromosome 15.

Researchers involved in the five-year study, which tested DNA samples from 1,200 families from around the world, speculate that there may be five or six primary genes and as many as thirty other genes involved in autism, although they recognize that this number could be higher still. They concede that it is still very early to model the ways in which these genes might bring about autism.

Researchers also have shed light on early brain growth and autism. A 2007 study showed that boys with autism and spectrum disorders experienced sudden, rapid brain growth resulting from higher levels of two growth-related hormones before age two, which is about the time the symptoms of autism appear in children. In this study, researchers identified growth in the cerebral cortex, an area where social, emotional, and language development occur. The researchers believe that the higher hormone levels might explain the greater head circumference seen in many children with autism. On another research front, scientists found that the risk of autism rises with the age of the father. According to the study, men who are forty and older are 50 percent more likely to have a child with autism than men in their twenties.

As researchers push the diagnosis envelope earlier and earlier through new findings about the causes of autism, another burgeoning area of study is emerging—designing interventions for infants.

▶ **FAST FACT**

While there is no general genetic test for autism, about 10 percent of all children with autism have an identifiable genetic disorder, such as fragile X or Rett's disorder. If your child is diagnosed with autism, you should request a genetic test (a blood test) to rule out these disorders.

You may have wanted a big family or at least another child. But your firstborn has been diagnosed with an autism spectrum disorder, and it's so much work that you can't fathom having another child. In time, you may change your mind. "What are the chances I'll have another child with an autism spectrum disorder?" is a question that genetic counselors can help you answer.

Although researchers and scientists have limited genetic information about autism, they know enough to calculate the risk and help you choose a course of action that is appropriate for your risk profile, family goals, and ethical and religious views.

Research reports put the risk of a sibling developing an autism spectrum disorder at between 3 and 7 percent. A clinic in the United Kingdom tells families that the risk is generally 5 percent, or 1 in 20. Another study says it could be as high as 18 percent. How the risk is expressed may seem high to one spouse and low to the other.

Genetic counseling involves gathering information about medical conditions and genetic disorders in your family, which helps determine the risk of having another child with a genetic disorder. To compile that information, use the My Family Health Portrait tool,* a service of U.S. Surgeon General's Family History Initiative.† This sophisticated, interactive tool lets you chart disorders in your family. When you're through, you can print out the chart, which looks like a family tree of health disorders, and show it to your genetic counselor. Genetic counselors also may ask questions about your distant relatives—great-aunts or second cousins—to further assess risk.

To learn more:

GenEdNet.org‡ is a general information site on genetics with links to consumer and educational resources.

Gene Clinics§ offers a voluntary listing of U.S. and international genetics clinics providing genetic evaluation and genetic counseling.

* https://familyhistory.hhs.gov
† www.hhs.gov/familyhistory
‡ www.genednet.org
§ www.geneclinics.org

GeneticAlliance* lists genetic disorders from A to Z. Autism and Asperger's disorder are listed in its Disease InfoSearch. Scroll through the list of disorders and click on "Autism." That will take you to a page that includes resources for autism, including a link to gene-testing literature.

* www.geneticalliance.org

▶ **INFORM YOURSELF**

The National Institutes of Health (NIH) support two major research networks dedicated to understanding and treating autism. NIH's Autism Research Network[†] is the main portal that connects the two networks—the Studies to Advance Autism Research and Treatment Network and the Collaborative Programs of Excellence in Autism Network. Each network branches out to include major universities across the country. Autism Speaks,[‡] which merged with Cure Autism Now[§] and the National Alliance of Autism Research, is a major powerhouse in the nonprofit sector to find a cure for autism.

Parents can get involved through IAN, the Interactive Autism Network,[**] a project of the Kennedy Krieger Institute and funded by Autism Speaks. IAN connects parents to researchers and matches them with clinical trials. Members of the IAN community also can ask questions about research and learn about new research findings. ClincialTrials.gov is another online source to find clinical trials in autism.

[†] www.autismresearchnetwork.org/AN
[‡] www.autismspeaks.org
[§] www.cureautismnow.org
[**] www.ianproject.org

SIX

▶ ▶ ▶ **Promising Treatments**

My social worker and I looked for landmarks and soon spotted the high chain-link fence that bordered the perimeter of the recreation yard at the rear of the Hope School in rural upstate New York. To some, the fence might have given a prisonlike appearance to the school, which educated children with autism. But these children don't play in a pack when they're outside; they sometimes wander off aimlessly until the hand of an adult reaches for their shoulder and pulls them back, or they bolt furiously away without provocation. Some wander away unnoticed and are discovered dead in nearby ponds. The fence was a good precaution.

We entered the school through a set of double glass doors, which led to a small lobby with industrial tile floors and expressionless walls. There was an almost perfect stillness instead of children laughing and skipping down the hallway. The director of the program led us into a room with a honeycomb of miniature drab-gray office cubicles, which were monitored by video cameras, not for security purposes but to make sure a therapist was doing her job. We sat off to the side to observe a child sitting in a small chair at a table, ready to start a therapy session in one of the cubicles.

Seated at a table across from five-year-old Ben, a small child with brown hair, a therapist opened her three-ring binder to look over a list of skills she would be teaching.

"Point to yellow," the therapist commanded, showing Ben a piece of paper with a big yellow dot on it. "Point to yellow."

He didn't have to make a choice; there was just one colored dot on the paper. He just had to point.

"Point to yellow," she said again, this time using her own finger to show Ben what to do. "Point to yellow."

When Ben didn't respond, she grasped his hand and placed it on the yellow dot. The next time Ben complied, and the therapist burst into life with a squeal of praise. "Good job, Ben. Good job."

She fed him a cracker, circled a plus sign on a chart, and then ran her finger down a list to remind her of what skill to teach next. For nearly an hour, Ben sat across from the therapist as she painstakingly instructed him to look into her eyes, wave his hand to say hello, touch his knee and then clap his hand, called a " two-step action." Each time Ben got it right, he got his reward. This was "work," a term the school used with the children when it was their time to leave the classroom and pull up a chair.

The director then led us to her office to show us progress reports. With the click of a mouse, she graphed the data collected from a child's responses over the course of several months. It showed a line trending upward, a sign of positive progress. But seeing the chart reinforced my distaste. This might be the right approach for some, but I did not want to imagine that my son's life would be charted with lines and numbers rather than with pen marks on a growth chart or hand prints in plaster.

Applied Behavior Analysis

The intervention strategy practiced by the Hope School is a form of applied behavior analysis (ABA), called discrete trial training (DTT) or the "Lovaas" approach. Nowadays, you'll hear ABA referred to as Intensive Behavioral Intervention (IBI), or Early Intensive Behavioral Intervention (EIBI). IBI or EIBI is the new euphemism for applied behavior analysis because it has less of a negative connotation than ABA, which is often misunderstood to mean DTT. ABA is an educational strategy for changing behaviors through positive reinforcement. DTT is one of several methods that use this strategy.

Psychologist O. Ivar Lovaas developed DTT in the 1960s for a program that involved up to forty hours of one-on-one instruction a week and which lasted, in some cases, for several years. Discrete trial breaks up skills into their tiniest parts, with each one taught individually in "trials," repeating the action over and over again, until each part of the skill is mastered. When a child complies, as Ben did when he finally pointed, a reward is given, which doesn't have to be something to eat. The reward could be praise, a hug, a favorite toy. It depends on what motivates the child.

At the time, I thought discrete trial training was the only kind of ABA. To me, its structured nature sounded unappealing, and it was maddening to think that I might need to use the technique to teach Leo how to respond to "How was your day?" While learning that response is standard for all humans, I didn't like the idea of teaching him a rote and robotic response. Instead, I wanted his response to reflect his true feelings, and on a deeper lever, I could not imagine how ABA could teach curiosity and creativity.

I do not believe anyone can teach these qualities. But I thought I could create an environment that would instill in Leo a desire to ask questions and explore answers. To do that, he would need to relate to me and others. These thoughts overwhelmed me.

Applied Verbal Behavior

I searched for another approach—one that relied less on repetition—and found it in applied verbal behavior (AVB). AVB was still grounded in the principles of behaviorism for teaching isolated skills, particularly language, but did so in the course of everyday activities rather than on a table top, as at the Hope School.

To learn this technique, I found a psychologist and read books with wordy titles, *Teaching Language to Children with Autism or Other Developmental Disabilities* and *The Assessment of Basic Language and Learning Skills (The ABLLS)*, pronounced *Ables*, both by Drs. James W. Partington and Mark L. Sundberg.[6] I slowly began to understand just how consequences shaped behavior, both positive and negative. Behaviorist B. F. Skinner was the pioneer. In 1930, Skinner built a contraption and let rats bounce around in it until they learned that if they pressed a lever, they could get a reward. Skinner applied this work to study the function of language—how we use words rather than how we compose a grammatically correct sentence—which led to his 1957 book *Verbal Behavior*, on which *The ABLLS* is based. And that's what applied verbal behavior teaches—the meaning of words, depending on their functions, or how they're used. For example, one word, such as "rose" may have multiple meanings, depending on whether you ask for it, identify it, or respond to a question about it. These are its functions.

I could understand some of the theory behind AVB but got lost in equations and a deeper explanation of the precepts of behavior modification. But the psychologist who taught me AVB said to just have fun with Leo, and that's what I did. I made a list of his "reinforcers"—Thomas the Tank Engine trains, water balloons, his baby blanket, chocolate—and kept them close at hand, pulling them out to motivate him to say a word, ask a question, or just express himself. I was always on the lookout for new reinforcers since his changed from month to month.

One day, while shopping at Wal-Mart, I discovered confetti poppers—little, square plastic bags filled with tissue-paper flecks of colored paper. Leo fell in love with confetti poppers. I'd blow one up with a built-in straw and then squeeze it in my hand until it exploded, showering the room with paper. I had Jamie, a home-based therapist, store them in the carpenter's apron I made her wear and pull them out to develop Leo's joint attention. She got Leo to look at the bag, then back at her, and back to the bag in anticipation of it popping.

"Leo, what do you want?" Jamie said.

She blew up the bag, waiting for Leo to respond. He looked at her but didn't speak.

"Leo, what do you want?" she said again. A few seconds passed with no response.

"Pop," said Leo.

Jamie squeezed her hand and burst the bag. The confetti fell to the ground like colored rain. She let out a cheer.

Leo's eyes got big. He moved closer to Jamie and held out his arms to let the confetti touch his skin as the paper twirled to the ground. He bent over to scoop up some confetti.

Jamie kneeled beside him. "Leo, what do you want?"

"Give him the echoic prompt," I said from the hallway, video-taping her.

"I want more confetti, Jamie. I want more confetti, Jamie," Jamie said. She wanted him to say these words.

▶ **FAST FACT** ─────────────────────────────

An echoic models a vocal sound, such as pronouncing the "b" sound in "ba." Answering a question is called an intraverbal. In many cases, intraverbals consist of just saying the next word in a sequence of words. Example: Row, row, row your [next word].

Leo ignored Jamie and focused on the confetti lying on the carpet. He scooped up a handful and then released the tiny scraps about six inches off the ground. Leo grabbed some more, rose to his feet, placed his hands directly in front of his eyes, and loosened his grip. Leo's eyes traced the paper drifting slowly downward.

"Show him," I said.

Jamie lowered her hands to show him another confetti popper. Leo was about to take it from Jamie when she pulled it away.

"I want confetti, Jamie," Leo said in a parrot-back fashion with his eyes directed at Jamie's waist instead of her face.

"Leo, what do you want?" Jamie said.

By this time, Jamie had Leo's attention. He tilted his head up and looked at her. "Blow it up," he said. "I want pop."

Jamie complied and depressed the lever of a hand tally to record Leo's mand, or request.

She continued to blow up and burst confetti poppers for as long as Leo desired the activity. This type of repetition was acceptable in AVB because Jamie was following Leo's lead and not imposing the activity on him. When he tired of it, she pulled something else out of her carpenter's apron with pockets kept full of reinforcers close at hand.

If he was watching TV, I'd stand in front of the TV and say, "Leo, what do you want?" and then give him the answer, "Say, 'Mommy move.'" I'd also turn off the TV and get him to say, "TV on," or I'd put a pillow in front of the screen, prompting him to say, "Move pillow." When he complied, he got a reward—a big hug, an M&M, a kiss. Leo responded favorably to AVB, partly because his echolalia made it easier for him to repeat words when I prompted him. But at the time, I didn't make that logical connection and thought Leo was truly talking.

As I got good at AVB, Leo and I had a blast. I let Leo do things that Mom would have never let me do as a child, such as cracking eggs. While he and I were making cookies, each step in the recipe offered a moment of instruction; I taught Leo to identify the cup, spoon, flour, and sugar and to define actions, such as stir, stir fast, stir slow, and crack an egg.

Leo always wanted to crack more eggs. At first I thought, no, cracking eggs wastes food, and I reactively pulled the egg carton out of his reach. But then I analyzed the benefit. Cost of eggs: about a dollar a carton. Benefit: Leo learns to say a new word, create a sentence, and we interact. We cracked a lot of eggs that spring. As Leo grew older, I let him peel off the tabs protecting the adhesive part of Band-Aids because it helped improve his fine motor skills. We went through a lot of Band-Aids, too; they cost more but not nearly as much as his other therapies.

Using ABA to Toilet Train

I then applied ABA principles to toilet training. Leo was almost four and a half, and I was tired of changing diapers and spending money on them. A year earlier, I had made my first attempt to toilet train Leo, spending more than a hundred dollars on toilet-training gizmos: books, videos, a soft potty training seat for the adult toilet, a portable potty, floating toilet targets. If the local baby store sold it, I bought it. In desperation, I called a local potty-training expert who'd written a book, but she never called me back. I filled out charts, noting when he soiled his diaper. I also collected data on the times that Leo urinated in his diaper. With this data, I'd sit him on the toilet around these times in the hope that he'd actually urinate in there. If he sat on the toilet for the desired number of minutes, I'd reinforce that behavior with M&M's.

That textbook approach to toilet training didn't work, so I gave up. As with any skill, if Leo wouldn't comply or show interest, I'd revisit it later. Sometimes I'd wait four to six months before trying again. I waited another year before I went back to toilet training.

When I first tried, I don't think he was developmentally ready. At four, I again drew on my knowledge of behavior modification and hit upon an idea that finally worked. Using Leo's attraction for cause and effect, I introduced blue food coloring into the toilet, which would turn green when urine mixed with it.

"Leo, watch this," I said. Drops of blue food coloring fell into the water. I sat down and urinated, rising as fast as I could to show him that the water had turned green. His interest peaked, but it took a few more times before he caught on and tried it himself. When blue food coloring lost its appeal, I used red and then other biodegradable food products. I squirted Reddi-whip into the bowl, telling Leo to "break up the iceberg!" Before long, I was dumping Apple Jacks cereal and anything else that wouldn't clog the pipes.

Mission half-accomplished. Two months later, Leo still couldn't control his bowel movements. We were into size five Huggies, and five weeks remained before the start of St. Columba's Nursery School. Although St. Columba's didn't require that he be toilet-trained, I knew that most of the other children entering their second year at the school would be in underwear, and the thought of being the only parent whose child was still in diapers mortified me.

That changed on the day I spaced out and forgot to put a diaper on him when I dropped him off at Basic Concepts, a therapeutic summer camp he was attending. As usual, I used the trunk of the car as a portable changing table, but left in a hurry, forgetting to put on a new diaper. The lead teacher called me later in the day, asking if I had done that on purpose. I immediately thought. "Oh no. Did he have an accident?" He didn't.

The next day, I wasn't sure whether I should put him back in a diaper or hope the training had worked. Not knowing what to do was a source of anxiety for the next two weeks. I diapered him for bed. He kept waking up dry, and he didn't have any accidents during the day. Patience paid off. Leo never used a diaper again, and if he had a rare accident, it was because he'd held in his urine too long.

Floortime

After eight months of an intensive applied verbal behavior program, a relatively short time compared to the experiences of other parents, I eased back and once again shifted the focus of his intervention plan to reflect his changing needs. After two-and-a-half years, I realized that children with autism often have so many needs that there is no one treatment that will address all of them. Moreover, I realized that whatever therapies made the most sense for Leo also needed to be reinforced by his educational environment. Any parent going through this needs to recognize and understand their child's needs in order to pick the right treatments and school program. This was an important concept for me to learn, but I can't honestly say I always looked at the big picture.

I often focused on just his language, as that delighted me when he began to express himself more spontaneously and ask questions. His beginning questions were simple. "Where's my dinosaur?" Then he took an interest in asking "what" and then "who" questions. The "hows" and "whys" were the last to come. He dropped the echolalia because he lost the need for it. He knew how to use words appropriately to create an original sentence and not rely on parroting chunks of words he had remembered from books or videos to communicate his desires.

Although verbal behavior was less important, I kept occupational therapy (OT) as a cornerstone of his intervention program because Leo still struggled with recognizing his own body space and relating to objects in space. These problems made it difficult for him to engage in common childhood activities, such as catching a ball or playing tag. Through OT, his therapist addressed these needs by strengthening his sensory-motor and visual-spatial development.

Recognizing Leo's emerging strength in language and symbolic play skills was the reason I shifted his intervention plan from a behavioral model to a developmental approach. The clear treatment choice was Floortime, an aptly named therapy that means what it says: Get down on the floor and play with your child. The activity didn't matter; what mattered was getting an interaction—the return of a smile, the to-and-fro of a conversation—things that come effortlessly to typical children. Floortime helped him through each developmental stage while appreciating his need to be more emotionally aware.

To learn Floortime, I enlisted the expertise of Dr. Serena Wieder, one of the cocreators of Floortime and coauthor of *The Child with Special Needs*, a book I read with the dedication of a nun—especially the part about how social interactions and communication flower from the natural development of emotions as a baby grows into a toddler and then a young child.

I was fascinated to learn that a baby's ability to identify and manage emotions in response to the outside world was the vital compound that promoted social and cognitive development. If emotional growth were stunted, then a baby's development would be thrown off course. None of the parenting tomes I had read made this point. I discovered that Floortime was as much a technique as it was a philosophy to embrace.

From the very moment a baby is born, language and communication skills begin to develop. The earliest skill—a baby's ability to calm itself in the face of distress—seems an unlikely candidate for promoting a gestural dialogue, but it is, according to the Floortime theory. A baby first must learn to soothe itself before it can engage in gestures. The baby learns how to do this through the thousands of interactions it experiences during its first three months of life. (A baby cries; a caregiver responds; the baby's needs are met; and the baby feels calmed.) A baby must master this skill—one of six skills in the development of emotions—before it can achieve mastery of subsequent skills. (See Table 1, pages 49–50.)

Just as crawling leads to walking and walking to running, emotional development has its own set of prerequisites for growth.

Each ring grows outward like the rings on a tree and is dependent on the growth of the previous ring, providing a solid foundation for future overall development until maximum growth is achieved. The consistent growth of these emotional milestones is critical because it allows a child to communicate, relate to others, and solve problems. Dr. Wieder told me during one of our Floortime sessions that mastery of these milestones was critical to Leo's emotional and intellectual growth.

If a ring is missing or fails to develop properly, then a baby lives and grows in a distressed world. Sometimes emotions do not develop because there are other developmental problems, particularly in planning motor actions. A child may appear clumsy or repeat arm movements—hand clapping, for example—because she is unable to sequence events.

Another common problem involves poor processing of outside stimuli from the five senses, which is known as sensory integration dysfunction (SDI), a term coined in the 1960s by A. Jean Ayres, an occupational therapist in California who believed that sensory processing difficulties interferes with learning. (SDI is now referred to as Sensory Processing Disorder.) This occurs because the neural networks in a child's brain aren't working properly. SDI manifests in a variety of ways. It can interfere with a child's ability to "shift gears" when faced with disappointment or to transition from one activity to another. For example, a child with SDI may react to a request to stop an activity with an explosive outburst, when a normal child, while disappointed, would simply move on. It is not uncommon for a child diagnosed with an autism spectrum disorder to have a sensory processing disorder, but a child with a processing disorder does not necessarily have autism.

Because the rings grow as a result of these interactions during the very early years of life, the Floortime approach reasons that the way to recapture the growth of lost or poorly developed rings is through persistent and joyful play that leads to a continuous flow of back-and-forth interactions between a child and an adult. That is the ultimate goal of Floortime, to "open and close" what Floortime calls "circles of communication."

A baby's ability to self-soothe leads to a growing awareness of the surrounding world and allows the baby between three and six months to form warm and trusting emotional connections to caregivers. After establishing this second ring, a baby begins to engage in gestural dialogues with caregivers, a form of two-way communication, which is the third ring. At a rudimentary level, these gestures occur by nine months and take the form of cooing, turning to look, and head nodding. They are the earliest examples of "circles of communication."

Out of the union of these rings, interactions become more complex and so does communication. This fourth ring—complex communication—allows a toddler to put reason to work to solve a problem. A toddler begins to understand that banging on the refrigerator door will attract the attention of a caregiver to fulfill his needs, which, in this example, could be juice. Toddlers develop this capacity between a year and eighteen months.

With this skill mastered comes the ability of toddlers, typically between the ages of two years and thirty months, to use ideas constructively to meet needs—asking for a cookie, for instance—or creatively in pretend play—feeding a dolly, for example.

The sixth and last ring involves making associations between ideas, or thinking logically. An example of this would be if a child says, "I want to play ball," and you say, "Why?" and the child responds, "Because I like to catch." Thirty minutes or so of Floortime five times or more each day helps a child master these six developmental milestones that he or she has missed since birth.

When I read about the stages in a child's emotional development, I had trouble understanding what I specifically needed to do to help Leo master them. I could never remember key points, what milestones to teach, how to teach them, which ones Leo had mastered, or how I could tell if he was achieving mastery. I didn't quite get it.

I understood that applied verbal behavior stood in stark contrast to Floortime from a clinical perspective, but when I was on the floor with Leo, the theory broke down. According to Floortime, the point was to play, to engage, to help Leo enjoy the real world and not just the world that existed from within, whereas AVB focused more on teaching isolated skills but in a naturalistic environment and with the same exaggerated facial expressions and body movements, known as "affect."

Dr. Wieder compared Floortime to strengthening the trunk of a tree, while applied verbal behavior merely strengthened its branches.

She took a genuine interest in Leo's case, and on that first visit in February 2001, she had uncanny insight and intuition about Leo. She told me that language and cognition would become Leo's strengths. I didn't know how she knew that, but I trusted her.

In her Floortime room, Leo gravitated to her train toys. At home, I had relegated his Thomas the Tank Engine train table to the basement. He constantly played with his trains, and sometimes he'd even clutch a train en route to speech therapy. Leo's therapists said he "perseverated" on his trains. The dictionary defines "perseverate" as an "action that recurs persistently." The way "perseverated" stuck in my mouth made me want to spit it out of my vocabulary. I tried not to make a big deal about the train. If I tried to pry it loose from his hand, he'd cry, and it wasn't worth it to make a scene.

I have nothing against trains, but I couldn't wait for the day I could banish the whole Thomas crew to the shed in the backyard. Leo's obsession with trains made the hair on my skin stiffen. I spoke with a mother of a nine-year-old boy with autism who said her son was stuck in this fantasy train world and wouldn't move on to more realistic play, as normal children do when they get older. I couldn't shake the image of Leo as a gangly, pimple-faced youth running to the train table at Toys "R" Us when the other children playing alongside him would still be in diapers. I'd be embarrassed once again. Hoping to push his development so that he'd separate fantasy from reality, I hid his trains in the hope that he'd find something else to play with, but he'd just ferret them out like a squirrel searching for buried nuts.

Dr. Wieder didn't find the trains as upsetting as I did. She engaged Leo in play with his trains as I observed in awe. "Leo, there's no driver in the train. The train needs a driver," she'd say. Since children on the spectrum struggle with abstract and logical thinking, she pushed him to stop and think, often challenging him in counterintuitive ways. Instead of telling Leo not to do something, she turned it around and asked him a question: "Why don't you want to do [and then fill in the blank]?" In time, Leo would challenge Dr. Wieder. If a train didn't have a driver, he said it was a "ghost train."

In Syracuse, the linchpin of Leo's therapy consisted of Floortime and sensory integration therapy, a type of occupational therapy that aims to correct underlying sensory deficits in order to boost the capacity for learning rather than to teach a specific skill, such as using scissors.

Leo's therapists in Syracuse practiced Floortime and led me to believe that I had to choose ABA over Floortime, as if it were an "either-or" decision. They didn't give me a scientific discourse on whether Floortime or any of the other treatments were "empirically validated," nor did I want such a discussion. I hadn't taken any research courses in college, so I wouldn't have known that "empirically validated" meant to prove a therapy's effectiveness, any more than I would've understood that medications undergo the same kind of rigorous testing before they are sold at the drugstore. But in such a study, volunteers are randomly assigned either a placebo or the real drug to measure effectiveness. Now I understood why parents wouldn't want their child randomly assigned a therapy that might be the equivalent of a placebo. Who would? I wanted the real thing, whatever that was, from the get-go. The good news is that science has advanced to the point where children are not denied treatment during research.

After Leo's evaluation at Yale in December 2000, I swung to behaviorism because the experts there said ABA had the best science behind it. They said treatment sessions could occur during the course of everyday activities that interested Leo rather than me drilling him at a table using activities I had chosen. I immersed myself in learning more about this "natural" way. It was called applied verbal behavior (AVB) and seemed easier to learn than Floortime. It required setting goals and defining skills, writing them down, and then grading Leo on whether he responded or not. I could see and measure progress, which encouraged me to continue the program.

Floortime Versus Applied Verbal Behavior

If I were reading a board book to Leo during an AVB session, we might cuddle on the coach while I prompted him to turn the page: "Leo, turn page." If he didn't turn the page, I'd show, then help him. Then I'd point to the first animal and say its name. I'd ask Leo to point to the animal and say, "Can you say 'cat'?" If Leo complied, I acknowledged his success with praise and might say something like, "Good talking. You said that word so nicely. Leo, do you see the bird in the tree? Point to the bird. Good boy! Is the bird on a high branch or a low branch? You're right! The bird is on a low branch."

If I were doing Floortime, I could also be reading the same book, but I wouldn't assume the role of task master while Leo played the role of learner. I'd find out what Leo might be interested in and work to develop a more equal partnership in conversation, much as in daily life encounters.

I'd let Leo explore the book, and if he took interest in an animal by making a suggestive sound or placing his hand on it (since he couldn't point very well), I'd say excitedly, "Oh, a cat!" and look in his eyes so he could see the worried expression on my face. If Leo didn't notice the bird, I might say, "Oh, no, a bird! Fly away, bird. The cat's going to chase you," and then I'd let out a big meow. I'd then say, "Fly, bird, fly." If Leo waved his arms, I'd wave mine, too. If Leo said, "Tweet, tweet," I'd develop a "tweet, tweet" dialogue with him. Or if he wanted to crawl off my lap and run around the house with me pretending to be a big chicken, I'd assume that role.

Our interaction would be characterized more by laughter, distinctive and exaggerated facial expressions and gestures, pleasurable tickles, stroking, and tender moments. I'd join Leo in the interaction and trade the lead back and forth, rather than dominate it, so that the emphasis was on Leo enjoying the fun of the social contact rather than showing me what he knew.

As I became secure in understanding both approaches, I could more clearly see their benefits. But I relied more on AVB since it was hard to have a back-and-forth interaction with Leo; he didn't stick with one activity for very long, and his ability to reason and express himself verbally was poor. Nonetheless, I tried to incorporate elements from Floortime when I played with him.

According to AVB instruction, I'd get Leo to say words; describe actions, tastes, and smells; or tell me the answers to questions I'd taught him. I gave Leo praise, big hugs, or M&M's when he did a good job. I borrowed elements of Floortime I found useful in challenging, arguing, and debating with Leo when he began to talk more fluently. For example, we once built a zoo out of blocks and plastic animals. Leo placed a lion in the same cage as a monkey. "Oh, no, Leo," I said in a shaky, quivering voice. "What's going to happen to the monkey if you leave him in with the lion?" I'd pick up the lion and let out a roar, moving it closer to the monkey.

The point was to get Leo to think logically and to understand that actions have consequences. In reality, the monkey would be in a separate cage from the lion because, if not, the monkey would end up as the lion's dinner. If Leo couldn't make that logical connection, I'd help him problem solve or brainstorm a new idea to save the monkey's life.

As I think back, I might have structured his therapy program differently and focused on Floortime and his social and emotional development, rather than on getting Leo to talk, if I'd taken the time to reflect on the purpose of all his therapy, which was to develop a deeper relationship with my son so that he could one day form relationships with other people. But I couldn't find time for the reflection required to make sense of this. Where could I find the moments to reflect when therapy dominated our days? It would take another three years for me to understand that he needed more than language in order to develop the ability to feel and interact with others.

As it was, we rushed from one appointment to the next, and down-time was taken up with at-home therapy. I never felt as if I had done enough. It was an incredible juggling act as I struggled to prioritize treatments that the professionals had recommended. They urged me to see this person and then that person, and then when Leo got a little older, he needed to see someone else.

I felt exhausted keeping Leo in check doing all those Floortime and AVB sessions, and carting him to his OT and speech therapy appointments, which took up eight hours every day. I fretted about ignoring Lucas. I didn't resent other mothers except maybe in the beginning, but I was jealous of their easier lives, or at least how they seemed easier.

◄ PRACTICAL ADVICE ►

Applied Behavior Analysis

Sixty-five years ago, when the disorder known as autism got its name, if your child received this diagnosis there wasn't much you could do about it—you were resigned to having a child with a broken mind, a mental cripple who turned home into hell.

It would be another twenty years before applied behavior analysis—the first promising treatment for autism—emerged. Back then, a 1965 *Life* magazine article profiled Dr. Ivar Lovaas and his team of researchers at the University of California in Los Angeles who developed a treatment that alternated between shocking roughness and persistent and loving attention. It was based on the old-fashioned idea of rewarding good behavior when children are good and punishing them when they're bad. To test his theory, the researchers worked with four autistic children, from seven to nine years old.

At the time, the approach flew in the face of traditional psychiatric treatment, which was to find and treat a child's "core neurosis." Lovaas believed that if he could force a child to act normally on the outside, it would effect a genuine change in a child's behavior on the inside. For example, he pushed a child to go through the motions of paying attention because he believed that eventually the child would pay attention. When the child refused to comply,

▶ **FAST FACT**

Autism treatments fall into five main groups: (1) medication or pharmacological treatments, (2) special diets, (3) behavioral families, (4) educational programs, and (5) complementary and alternative medicine, called CAM treatments.

Always bear in mind one of the central conclusions of current research: The philosophy of the intervention programs vary as do their outcomes, but the critical components that go into a program share key elements. How early you start, how many hours you participate, the amount of family involvement and integration with typical peers, the level of team approach, and other variables are critical components. The staff of the Department of Psychology at the Autism Treatment Services of Canada drew on a corpus of research to come up with these components.

To you this means:

Age at which treatment is started. Move beyond the denial phase as quickly as you can. Numerous studies show that the younger a child is when treatment is begun, the more likely he or she is to make significant gains. This is perverse advice, but even before you know what you are doing or what you are up against, you should assume the worst and begin your battle against it.

Treatment intensity. There is almost no amount of therapeutic intervention that is too much. A number of studies show significant cognitive and behavioral gains with at least twenty-five hours of therapy each week. These results generally rest on the assumption that treatment is continuous over twenty-four months without summers off and is characterized by one-to-one or small-group instruction. Obviously, this huge commitment completely transforms your family.

Family involvement. Unlike a medical condition in which you turn your child over to the professionals for care, autism cannot be successfully addressed without parental engagement. Parental training—also involving other family members—keeps therapy going through the child's entire day and week. Without counsel from professionals, it is nearly impossible to devise viable coping strategies for anger, tantrums, rigidity, speech challenges, social isolation, and the full range of negative behaviors.

Inclusion with typical peers. Children mimic the behavior they observe. It is crucial that children on the spectrum interact with typically developing peers so they can develop more conventional behaviors and skills.[7] While this situation may meet with strong resistance from your child, don't think it is without effect even if he or she does not appear to be paying attention. This setting allows a child to generalize and apply the skills he or she is developing in an isolated treatment environment. Recruit children as "playdates" and let the chemistry sort itself out. While some children won't connect, you may find others who can engage with your child better than you can.

Diverse team members. The number of different professionals from different disciplines who can help your child can be overwhelming. Unfortunately, you can't simplify treatment by having one person treat your child. You'll need a crew because your child's needs are extremely diverse, and a range of professional competencies is necessary. The speech therapist cannot help in the way a psychiatrist can, who in turn cannot help you in the way a developmental pediatrician or occupational therapist can. Others who might play a vital role in your child's therapy include medical practitioners, psychologists, occupational therapists, physical therapists, teachers, and special education providers. Once you've carefully assembled this "multidisciplinary" team, you have to help them stay in touch with one another. A simple email list with a regular update—written by you—is probably enough; however, regulations in some states prohibit therapists to communicate with parents via email because of privacy concerns.

Success may be slow and of course is not guaranteed. But these elements of an effective approach are tried and tested and are good dimensions to use in order to plan and to evaluate your intervention. To download the report *Treatment Programs for Young Children with Autism: Identifying the Critical Program Elements*, visit the treatment service's site* and click on "Articles" to find it.

* www.autism.ca

Lovaas scolded and slapped the child. Further noncompliance meant a trip to the "shock room," where mild jolts of electricity passed through the child's bare feet.

He rewarded good behavior with food. Using this technique, he taught another child to ask for things by giving the child food every time the child said the right sound or word. The child didn't get anything if he made a mistake. It took some 90,000 "trials" for the child to learn how to talk. Work was interspersed with ten-minute "play breaks," during which Lovaas lavished the child with attention in the hope that it would eventually be returned.

In 1981, Dr. Lovaas published *Teaching Developmentally Disabled Children: The ME Book*, which was the only "parent-friendly" training manual that showed parents how to implement his behavioral intervention program. During the next sixteen years, applied behavior analysis evolved to more naturalistic techniques, rendering some of the techniques, particularly using shock therapy to punish bad behavior, obsolete. But the core feature of the program still calls for thirty to forty hours a week of intensive individual therapy.

Learn more: *www.lovaas.com*

DIR and Floortime

In 1992, Dr. Stanley Greenspan's book, *Infancy and Early Childhood: The Practice of Clinical Assessment*, brought Floortime to the fore, though Greenspan and cocreater Dr. Serena Wieder began using it on children with autism spectrum disorders in the mid-1980s. Floortime, or play therapy, as some refer to it, is a competing method to behaviorism and now the fastest growing intervention in the field, though ABA still dominates. Floortime emphasizes a child's emotional, social and imaginative abilities—autism's core deficits—and was developed from brain research that shows human development hinges on interactions and the relationships that develop from them.

Don't confuse the DIR (its full name is Developmental, Individual-Difference, Relationship-Based) model with Floortime and lump them together as one in the same. They are different, even though they are expressed as the DIR/Floortime model. Think of the DIR as the axis around which to organize your thoughts, looking at your child's unique challenges and strengths and then knowing which specific interventions to select as part of a comprehensive program. In other words, the DIR model provides the framework for determining which interventions are right for your child. The DIR model stresses six milestones of emotional development that children need to master before more advanced learning can occur. (See Table 1, pages 49–50.)

Floortime, on the other hand, is a specific technique that involves following your child's natural emotional interests and challenging him toward greater mastery of the six milestones. The technique is to get on the floor with a child and create opportunities for the child to master these milestones through interactive play. A tenet is to follow a child's lead, not dominate it. The process of play and developing an even flow of back-and-forth interactions is much more important than the specific activity you're engaged in. Ideally, Floortime requires an investment of six to ten sessions a day, with each session lasting twenty to thirty minutes. Its creators also recommend a very serious playdate program—at two, have two playdates a week; at three increase the number to three; and so on—then maintain as many as possible during the school years.

Learn more: *www.icdl.com*

Which Treatment Is Best for Your Child?

These two treatments have won broad acceptance by parents and practitioners, even though the quality of the scientific research behind them is still being debated. Saying one treatment is more effective than another triggers lively and heated debate among practitioners and researchers. Experts struggle with defining what it means to say a treatment has enough evidence behind it so that it earns the label of "effective," "scientifically valid," or " evidence-based."

According to a special panel of the American Psychological Association, no definitive research exists on any treatment for autism,[8] though applied behavior analysis (ABA) offers the best supporting evidence. The famous 1987 study by Dr. Lovaas cemented that belief. In that study, Lovaas compared three groups of children. The first group received forty hours of ABA a week, the second one received only ten hours of behavioral treatment along with a variety of other therapies, and the third group received no behavioral intervention. Dr. Lovaas published results showing that about half of the children who received intensive ABA therapy wound up in regular first grade classes, and their IQs jumped thirty points.

Critics, however, knock the rosy outcome. Lovaas did not randomly assign the children to treatment groups, as one would do in a controlled study, and his criteria for normalcy—normal-range IQ scores and placement in a regular school—could still apply to a child with autism. Despite the study's flaws, the National Institute of Mental Health lists ABA as the only documented effective treatment for autism. It cites *Mental Health: A Report of the Surgeon General*, which states that "thirty years of research demonstrated the efficacy of applied behavioral methods in reducing inappropriate behavior and in increasing communication, learning and appropriate social behavior."[9] Other backers include the American Academy of Pediatrics and the National Research Council, a panel of experts convened by the federal government to look at the research, which led to the council's 2001 report, *Educating Children with Autism*.

The prickly issue over the efficacy, or effectiveness, persists because no treatment has undergone the gold standard of testing—double-blind trials. Double blind means that neither the patients nor clinical investigators know who's receiving the actual treatment versus a placebo until the trial is over. This procedure creates unbiased results that can be replicated.

There are logical reasons why autism treatments lack this high standard of scientific rigor. No parent would want a child randomly assigned to treatment, especially if it means stopping another treatment during testing.

But that doesn't mean that no research exists. Studies on the effectiveness, ineffectiveness—and harm—of autism treatments span more than three decades. What exist, however, are mainly doctors revisiting their patients after many years of treatment and reviewing their charts, or small or single-subject studies that often do not sample the true population of children with autism. In some of these studies, positive results may be stressed while negative points get buried. That leaves practitioners in a position of relying on the *strength* of the scientific evidence to determine which treatment might work.

When the experts can't agree on the effectiveness of treatments, it makes your job of sorting through this thicket even more daunting. Choosing the "best" treatment is relative, because what's best for one child may not be best for your child. In developing an intervention program, think of it as a framework that defines and targets goals for your child. Often choosing a treatment is not an "either-or" decision. You'll want treatments that will target all areas of your child's development—communication, social skills, play, cognition, and imagination.

▶ **FAST FACT**

According to the late Donald J. Cohen, former director of the Yale Child Study Center, "When there is no cure, there are 1,000 treatments." Indeed. Research Autism* has compiled a list of more than 500 autism treatments, which is perhaps the most comprehensive list available. Some interventions are rated using a scale that ranges from "very strong positive evidence" to "very strong evidence of harmful effects."

*www.researchautism.net/pages/interventions/alphabetic

As you explore treatments, stay focused. Look at your child's strengths and challenges—and the purpose of intervening, which is to help your child develop meaningful relationships, communicate appropriately, and improve undesirable behaviors. Once you and the experts identify your child's goals, choosing treatments to redirect the course of your child's development should come into sharper focus.

Despite the support behind ABA, parents often shy away from it because of its negative portrayal in the media. "Drill-like," "robotic," and "mechanistic" are common descriptors. That certainly was the approach when ABA emerged in the 1960s with discrete trial training.

However, newer methods, such as applied verbal behavior, or AVB, teach skills without drills and in a child's everyday environment rather than at a table. See on page 125 to understand this method and how it differs from ABA.

TEACCH

Another treatment with strong heuristic evidence—and huge followings—is TEACCH, which stands for Treatment and Education of Autistic and related Communication-handicapped CHildren. According to the National Research Council's report, Floortime

▶ **FAST FACT** ——————————————————————————

Families today try as many as nine and use between four and six different treatments, mainly speech and occupational therapy, a picture exchange program, sensory integration therapy, ABA, social skills training, Floortime, and music therapy, according to one study.[10] And they are constantly on the lookout for anything else that might help their child.

and TEACCH offer some supporting evidence. TEACCH is one of the oldest and most widely used program in North Carolina schools. Developed in the 1970s at the University of North Carolina, the long-term goal of TEACCH is to help children develop as many key life skills as possible for independent living. The method, another spin on behaviorism, emphasizes instruction that teaches to the strengths of most children with autism—their visual skills. Classroom and home environments are arranged with clear, concrete visual information. In the classroom, trained teachers keep children focused and interacting through pictures, schedules, and visual cues. For example, if a child is told to "wait," the child could be taught to go to a "blue" carpet square and sit. Providing a visual cue is likely to make more sense to a child with autism than the abstract concept of waiting. Small-group and one-on-one instruction are provided. Parents, acting as cotherapists, support and reinforce classroom instruction through a home program. TEACCH, which is provided free throughout the state, is not exclusive to North Carolina; other schools across the nation have adopted its techniques.

Learn more: *www.teacch.com*

Understanding the Difference Between the Lovaas Approach and Applied Verbal Behavior

Applied behavior analysis is an educational strategy, not a therapeutic technique. The most publicized technique that uses ABA principles is discrete trial training (DTT), which has become synonymous with the Lovaas approach and gets all the media attention.

The Lovaas approach teaches language in this concrete, rote, and drill-like fashion. The premise is that children should learn to understand what is said to them (receptive language) and comply if a request is made (point to the cookie). A problem with this approach is that a child may be able to identify objects but not know how to ask for one. This is because the child may have difficulty associating the desire for, say, eating a cookie with the word itself.

A newer technique—applied verbal behavior, or AVB—addresses this limitation and flips the reasoning for how language should be taught. AVB emphasizes expressive communication by teaching a child that a word has meaning across a variety of situations. If the child understands the connection between a word and the value held by its meaning, the child will learn how to express his desires and needs to get them fulfilled. To accomplish that, AVB takes a cue from Floortime, which is to capture a child's imagination by noticing the child's interests. These interests serve as a starting point for teaching the child to ask for things, and that's where AVB and Floortime diverge. AVB is a language and communication program; Floortime is not.

Applied verbal behavior is derived from B. F. Skinner's 1957

▶ **FAST FACT**

Relationship Development Intervention. In the scheme of interventions, relationship development intervention, or RDI[‡] is one of the newer autism treatments. RDI doesn't seek to alter behavior like ABA but focuses on strengthening emotional skills that infants learn on their way to childhood. These skills include forming loving relationships, empathy, compassion, and sharing joy with others. Dr. Steven Gutstein, a clinical psychologist and founder of the ConnectionsCenter in Houston, Texas, developed RDI, which has been compared to other developmental interventions, such as Floortime. RDI offers a great line of reasoning: If you strengthen emotional connections in the brain, then a child will be more motivated to engage in and enjoy social relationships. As with many interventions, no studies prove its effectiveness as an evidence-based treatment. RDI is also very expensive.

[‡] www.rdiconnect.com

book, *Verbal Behavior.* Drs. James W. Partington and Mark L. Sundberg took that theory and developed a tool that evaluates language and communication deficits in children from three to nine years old. The ABLLS, which stands for the *Assessment of Basic Language and Learning Skills,* is the product of their research. This tool, which has been revised, is also used to develop a curriculum for teaching language and other communication skills. The intensity of AVB—at least twenty-five hours a week—is the same as with other ABA programs. Which intervention plan—DTT, AVB, or some other behavior approach—is the correct one for your child will depend on his or her unique challenges.

Learn more:

▸ Behavior Analysts Inc.:* Primary source on applied verbal behavior information.

▸ Cambridge Center for Behavioral Studies:† Explains behavior analysis in clear language.

▸ Association for Behavior Analysis International:‡ International organization for professionals and students of behavior analysis. Showcases publications, events, and professional conferences.

How to Find and Train Student Therapists

Parents want to be their child's frontline therapists, but that is tremendously challenging and, one might say, close to impossible. You and your child have a highly nuanced relationship that can

---

* www.behavioranalysts.com
† www.behavior.org/autism
‡ www.abainternational.org

never be exclusively focused on therapy. In a number of therapeutic programs, it is just impossible for one person to handle the number of hours necessary. Finally, your child probably benefits from having therapists who present a somewhat different dynamic to adjust to. A home-based program, for example, requires a parent to locate, hire, train, supervise, and pay student therapists, though a growing number of services exist that will do that for you.

Using student therapists can benefit both you and the students. You get an energetic individual who is eager to help with all those sessions demanded by home-based programs—and save money. A student therapist costs a fraction of securing the services of a licensed therapist.

Look for colleges, community colleges, and universities in your area that offer courses in psychology, special education, and speech-language pathology to find student therapists. Search the Web to find university websites and then drill down to find these departments. Look for a phone number. Despite the ease of email, make the phone call. That way you'll know whether you got through. With email, your message might be routed to a spam filter or diverted to a public mailbox and never reach its recipient. Moreover, you can't be sure that the email addresses on a website are kept current. When you find a phone number, you don't need to talk to the department head. The assistant will have more time for you. Call and ask that person whether the department offers a listserv, or email discussion list, for its students. If it does, you're halfway there.

Get the name and phone number of the listserv administrator and call that person. Here's a sample script: "I'm [your name], and I'm the mother of a child with special needs. I'd like to find a student therapist. I understand you're in charge of the listserv. Would you post an announcement for me on your discussion list?" If the listserv administrator agrees, ask for his or her email address and permission to send your announcement for posting.

If the college does not have a listserv for its students, find the professors who teach speech-language pathology or what's called "abnormal psychology," a course typically taught to undergraduate psychology majors. Call these professors and ask them if they'd announce your ad to their class. If you don't live near a university, consider hiring grandmothers. They've got a lot to give and might do it for free.

Composing the Ad: What to Say

Your ad should be ready to go once you contact the person who is willing to post it. You don't want to wait days between the time the listserv administrator offers to post your ad and when you send it. In your ad, describe your child's disability and mention the diagnosis if you feel comfortable with divulging that information. Outline the student's job responsibilities as clearly as possible. This sample ad got results. Adapt it to your needs.

Your ad should offer training by a certified professional, such as a psychologist, speech-language pathologist, or a board certified behavior analyst (BCBA). Look for the BCBA credential after the

---

▶ **Social Skills Therapist Wanted**—Washington, DC: Seeking social skills therapist for bright and verbal 3½-year-old with developmental delays. Will train the right person. Ideal qualifications include a person who is highly animated, energetic but most of all dedicated and committed to helping a very special child. Responsibilities include facilitating social interactions with typically developing peers during one-on-one play dates, coming up with play activities that promote social interactions, and expanding play and conversation skills. Hours: Call to discuss. $10–$12/hour, depending on experience. Convenient location—5 blocks from Bethesda Metro stop. Contact: [name] at [email address] or [phone number].

name. A word about speech pathologists: They're not always trained to handle the behavior problems that often arise in an ABA program. Be prepared to seek the advice of a child psychologist.

Also, skip the details about hours and days in your ad. Leave that open for discussion with the students who respond. They have class schedules to work around. Be flexible. If you live near a subway or bus line, mention that. It is a big draw since many students don't have a car. Once your ad is posted to a listserv, you're likely to find several candidates to interview within the first three days.

Forget printing out an ad and posting it on a student bulletin board. That's a perfunctory exercise that is unlikely to yield any immediate results.

How Much Should You Pay

The cost of such a program is not difficult to determine—the prevailing wage rate times the number of weekly treatment hours your psychologist recommends. Students who know nothing about applied behavior analysis can be had for as little as $10 to $12 an hour. Hourly rates of $20 to $30 per hour are not uncommon, depending on the therapist's experience and your location. If you're not sure what to pay, and you do want to be fair, get some guidance from other parents or one of the professors you've called.

Picking the Right Student Therapist

Juniors, seniors, and graduate students are the best pool to pick from because they are the most mature, committed, and dedicated. You'll need at least two student therapists in a home-based program, one for the morning shift and one for the afternoon. Once you start getting responses to your ad, get their résumés, if they have one, and screen prospective students over the phone. If you don't connect with them right away, it's unlikely your child will. Invite the promising ones over to your house to meet your child and interact with him or her. A student can have the best grades, but if he or she lacks expression and energy, it won't do either of you any good. You're assessing personality and empathy, not academic achievement.

Once you select your crew, start training and allow them some time to get to know your child. It often takes at least a month for a student therapist to develop a rapport with your child. Try starting out one hour a day for two to three days a week, then increase the number of hours week by week until you've reached the recommended amount. You'll also be meeting weekly with your psychologist in the beginning to refine your child's goals. During this process, your child is constantly being evaluated through your feedback.

How to Set Up a Floortime and Sensory Room

The philosophy of Floortime is to interact with your child—anywhere and anytime an opportunity arises. Everyday moments—mealtime, bath time, dressing, and undressing—are prime opportunities for interaction. It doesn't matter what you do as long as you persist in your pursuit to engage your child. Pick up and go with her lead.

If your treatment plan calls for X number of Floortime sessions a day, then you might want to set up a special room and fill it with toys that lend themselves to interacting with your child at different developmental levels, force engagement and imagination, and appeal to the five senses. Many people use a spare room in their basement or attic. The size of the room depends on your child's sensory needs. Children who are more active are likely to need a bigger space.

Pick toys your child loves and that you think he is ready for. For example, if your child is at a basic level of engagement and enjoys toy trains, hide one in your hand and get your child to search for it. As your child builds skills, you can add other props. Consider a doctor's kit to fix dolls, which can nurture empathy. To engage in pretend play and build communication skills, use two telephones. During a pretend birthday party, wrap small gifts in Kleenex.

Cars that hold passengers can teach children to think logically. If your child drives the car off without a driver, you can ask, "Who's driving the car?" You also can use these opportunities to teach safety by saying, "The driver needs a seatbelt." Then use a rubber band as a seatbelt and wrap it around the driver to demonstrate this point.

▶ **INFORM YOURSELF** ————————————————————

Drs. Mark Sundberg and James Partington make presentations on applied verbal behavior but limit visits to the East Coast. Visit Behavior Analysts Inc.* for upcoming trainings. Dr. Vincent Carbone[†] and his associates also teach applied verbal behavior at workshops around the country. For free trainings, check with your local chapter of Parents of Autistic Children.[‡] Free trainings are offered in New Jersey and Pennsylvania.[§] The Pennsylvania Department of Education has developed a plain-English family handbook on applied verbal behavior.[**]

The Behavior Analyst Certification Board certifies individuals to oversee behavioral programming for children with autism. Parents can search the board's registry[††] to find certified behaviorists by last name, city, state, ZIP code, and mile radius.

For Floortime training, the Interdisciplinary Council on Developmental and Learning Disorders[‡‡] offers a six-day program for licensed professionals.

* www.behavioranalysts.com
[†] www.drcarbone.net
[‡] www.poac.net
[§] www.poacofpa.net
[**] www.pattan.k12.pa.us/files/autism/verbalbeh0106.pdf
[††] www.bacb.com/consum_frame.html
[‡‡] www.icdl.com/staging/providers/database/index.shtml

Action figures (pirates and knights are favorites) can help children problem solve and separate reality from fiction. If the knight flies on top of the castle, ask your child if this could really happen. Help your child work out the reasoning for their actions.

Monitor your child's reaction to see whether the activity is too simple, too complex, or too overwhelming. Don't get discouraged if your child doesn't use toys appropriately. Not all children can play with toys to create ideas and work on symbolic themes, and not all children choose toys. Often, difficulty in planning coordinated actions, known as motor planning, and poor visual-spatial skills, which relate to how the brain interprets what the eyes see, inhibit a child's ability to use toys creatively. So many of these children rely on just moving themselves in dress up and drama to express ideas and emotions. A Floortime room embraces all avenues of symbolic expression—using toys (when they turn into ideas), using drama, using movement, art, music and so on.

Sensory items to consider include a bubble tube, soft mats, a fiber-optic light source, beanbag chairs, disco ball and projector, small trampoline, mirrors, expandable tunnels, a mattress, or blankets draped over the arms of chairs to create a clubhouse. Paint the walls a pastel color; white looks too clinical, and take down any pictures or posters.

You can find material at hardware stores and online vendors, such as CoolStuffCheap,* which sells bubble tubes with changeable filters for under $70. eFooF.com sells chairs that look like beanbag chairs but are covered in velvet and filled with big chunks of polyurethane foam so they don't mat down as easily. Don't get vinyl; it's cold and uncomfortable.

CoolStuffCheap also sells inexpensive fiber-optic lighting. For a ball pit, use an old portable crib and fill it with small plastic balls the size of your fist (Toys "R" Us sells them in duffel bags of 100).

---

* www.coolstuffcheap.com

As a final addition, put shimmer curtains over the windows or walls. Try Premier Lighting and Production Co.* Southpaw Enterprises† sells therapeutic swings and other sensory products, such as fake snow that feels like the real thing when mixed with water.

You can get more ideas by visiting the websites of the companies that sell multisensory equipment, such as Rompa's online superstore‡ and Flaghouse.§

The Coping site** lists more props and play activities for Floortime.

As your child matures and if he is able to discuss feelings and ideas grounded in logic and reality, Floortime will then turn into "Talk Time."

▶ **FAST FACT** ───────────────────────────────

How far should you push your child? As your child begins treatment, you may ask yourself if pushing your child to "work" (even if you call it "play," it's still work) for five or more hours a day is too much for him to tolerate. But if you think about it for a moment, children actively explore their environment throughout the day, give or take a few naps. No one expects you to force your child to sit at a table for hours or participate in small-group instruction for more than ninety minutes—an eternity for a young child. Skills can be taught in less structured settings—on a walk, in the grocery store, in the bathtub, in a playroom. Let your child choose the environment to explore and set it up to foster interaction. Not every day will be a good day, however, and you may find that you both need a break. That's okay. Just make sure that if your child starts to cry or becomes aggressive, don't end a therapy session on such a negative note. Get your child to deliver a correct response, then end the session; otherwise, you'll reinforce bad behavior.

---

* www.premier-lighting.com
† southpawenterprises.com
‡ www.rompa.com
§ www.flaghouse.com
** www.coping.org/intervention/floortm.htm

SEVEN

▶ ▶ ▶ Alternative Therapies

The experts advised me not to get sidetracked by alternative therapies. They didn't have to say much to convince me that their advice was sound; I considered myself to be a scientific person. While growing up, I was skeptical of paranormal phenomena and, as an adult, never treated my ailments with herbs. That didn't mean I wasn't intrigued by the claims or didn't try them. My favorite home remedy came from Mom, who removed wood splinters in my hand with bacon fat; the bacon made the skin swell and dislodged the splinter.

But since I felt that I had only one shot at finding the right therapeutic program before the window to heal Leo closed, it made more sense to choose treatments grounded in science than based on anecdotes, simplistic studies, and ambiguous testimonials. Swimming with dolphins, enclosing my son in an oxygen chamber, steroids, antifungal medications, marijuana, healing crystals, megavitamins, light therapy, eliminating body toxins through chelation—they all seemed a waste of Leo's time and my limited resources, financial and emotional, not to mention weird.

Nonetheless, I tried them anyway. I was seduced, like so many parents are, by the promise of hope over the findings of science. It was haphazard and clumsy and messy and expensive and enervating, but I was absolutely haunted by the fear that *if I didn't do everything as soon as possible*, my child would not become an independent, functioning adult. I made therapeutic, educational, and financial decisions, as best I could, in this environment of continual crisis. I list these alternative therapies to give you a sense of what's out there. As with all treatments, do your homework as to the potential risks, listen to your trusted expert advisers, understand their biases toward treatments, protect your financial resources, and always pay close attention to how your child responds.

Wilbarger Brushing Protocol

My first experience was with the Wilbarger Brushing Protocol. It's fairly easy and cheap, but like all therapies, requires commitment.

Leo's occupational therapist recommended this body-brushing therapy, which was supposed to help Leo's brain organize the input of sensory information. Several times a day, I firmly stroked, in one direction, Leo's arms, legs, back, and the soles of his feet with a soft plastic brush meant for removing silk threads from husked corn, followed by compressing his joints with my hands. There were no immediate results, but I did it anyway.

Special Clothing

To further orient his body to his surroundings, I bought him a weighted vest filled with bags of granular shotgun pellets, the number of which was calculated at 5 percent of his body weight. The vest, which was secured with Velcro around his chest, applied deep pressure to his joints and was supposed to help him self-soothe and relax. I think it worked for a while, since he seemed less active, but I can't be sure. His teachers said they noticed a difference, but after Leo started to rip it off, I gave up on using it. The experts at Yale also discouraged its use, saying that the weight of the vest could unnecessarily tire Leo.

Auditory Integration Training

I then tried auditory integration training, which supposedly re-teaches the ear to listen and, in theory, improves listening, language skills, and behavior. I was gung-ho on trying the Tomatis Method, a form of auditory training that was developed in the early 1950s by French physician Dr. Alfred A. Tomatis. I had read the book *When Listening Comes Alive* by Paul Madaule, and was completely enamored of the idea that the Tomatis Method could retrain Leo's ears to listen better and respond to me and others. Yale recommended against listening therapy because of the unknown long-term impact of exposing the ear to synthesized music. The American Speech-Language-Hearing Association also did not find sufficient evidence that this therapy worked.

I tried it when I had a two-week gap of down time to fill between the end of a school program and the start of a summer speech camp. David called Tomatis "expensive babysitting" because Blue Cross and Blue Shield did not reimburse the $8,000 treatment. I now think David was right, but at the time I had convinced myself that Tomatis was a must-do therapy.

As part of the program, a therapist recorded my voice and mod-ulated its frequency spectrum. When she played it back, I sounded like frogs croaking. But the therapist said Leo would reconnect with my voice because this was how it would have sounded to him in my womb. At that point, I thought it was a bunch of hooey, but I went along with it because I had paid half of the fee in advance, and there were no refunds.

When we arrived for the sixth day of the training, I checked in with the receptionist and waited for Leo's therapist to come and get him. In the waiting room, I struck up a conversation with a middle-aged woman from India. I enjoyed chatting with other mothers, curious to know their experience with autism treatments. The mother, who had flown in from Atlanta with her teenage son, mentioned that she had had some success with chelation. I had attended a seminar about the unorthodox practice of chelation therapy, and it sounded like snake oil medicine. Chelation is supposed to remove lead and other toxic metals from the body, but the U.S. Food and Drug Administration hasn't approved any form of chelation to treat autism. Chelation was gaining in popularity after news reports broke linking the mercury content in vaccines as a contributing cause of autism. Some specialists suggested that children with autism undergo chelation to cleanse their bodies of this heavy metal.

The mother said she had detoxified her teenage son several times. I kept asking silent questions in my head: *Why have you chosen an invasive and potentially dangerous therapy? You could be destroying your son's brain cells. Why are you doing this?* But it was not my place to judge her. The feeling of hopelessness that can grow when you are raising a child with autism can feed feelings of desperation. To me, the "miracle" chelation treatment seemed like a last-resort therapy.

I don't know whether the Tomatis Method had any effect on Leo. I can't say it was a negative experience, since he slept through the night on the days he had therapy, and that was something. I tried it because I didn't want to wake up feeling guilty years later because I didn't try everything that could have helped Leo. I fell into the trap that if the therapy costs a lot, it must be good. But I now wish that I had used the money for more occupational and speech therapy.

Homeopathy

As Leo progressed, I continued to look for solutions to help him regulate his emotions. His uneven moods and reactions to disappointments perplexed me. Sometimes, he'd burst into tears if I cut his French Toaster Sticks with a knife instead of the neat snip of poultry shears. He didn't like the crumbs left by a knife and fork.

▶ **FAST FACT** ————————————————————————————————

Some parents who support the autism-vaccine link are turning to a controversial treatment, called chelation (pronounced *key-lay-shun*), to purge their child's body of mercury. Chelation is a process in which chemicals are injected into the bloodstream to cleanse the body of this heavy metal. The theory of chelation therapy is based on the belief that if you remove mercury from the body, then the symptoms of autism will lessen or go away. For more than forty years, chelation has been used to treat lead poisoning. But its effectiveness for treating children with autism has never been proven.

In 2006, the National Institutes of Health (NIH) decided to investigate the effectiveness of chelation to treat autism. The NIH clinical trial is the first controlled study on using chelation therapy for this purpose. Researchers will judge its effectiveness by observing whether social behavior improves in the children who received chelation.

Moreover, a "federal vaccine court" in Washington, DC, began hearing the first of nine cases to determine—from a legal perspective, not a scientific one—if mercury in common childhood vaccines causes autism. Nearly 5,000 families are part of this class-action lawsuit, which could award millions to them if the court rules in their favor.

Other times, he'd show flexibility, saying, "We'll use something else," if he couldn't find a particular LEGO part to build a character.

When I asked David if we should try medication, such as Prozac or Risperdal, it evoked strong emotions in him. "Getting him to take them will be yet another crisis. He'll be dependent on them for the rest of his life. They could change his personality. He'll stop eating . . ." and on and on.

"Yes, yes," I said. "All possible, but let's try."

"Medicate yourself," he said, "not Leo."

The discussion was left unresolved, and I began to investigate homeopathy. Homeopathy treats conditions with herbal and mineral formulas, called remedies, which are typically in the form of tiny sugar balls. I figured I could get Leo to comply because he liked sweet things. I knew that a homeopathic remedy wouldn't eliminate his frustrations, but it might allow him to handle them better.

The homeopath was known for treating children on the spectrum, with clients traveling from as far away as India for treatment. When someone tells you that, you think: *He must be good!* The homeopath also did phone consultations, which was the route I sought. During my consultation, I held back Leo's diagnosis, fearing that the label would influence his perception of my son and ensuing treatment recommendation. I'd learned my lesson to watch my words when I'd told all to the director of the university-run preschool for children with language delays, and she refused to consider Leo for her program. Leo attended the program after the morning session at St. Columba's Nursery School when he was four years old. Her reaction floored me because she based her decision on her reaction to the label. (I got her to reconsider inviting him in for a play session. He got in. The upside of anger, as they say.)

The homeopath asked routine intake questions, and I volunteered Leo's language and fine-motor delays. Then he switched topics and asked me my age.

"I'm forty-eight."

"Mrs. Lytel," he said. The tone of his voice deepened, and I knew the next words out of his mouth were about to redirect the conversation. *What had I said? Could he tell that I was skirting the truth about Leo?*

"I need to ask you this," he said. A long pause. "Did you want to have this child?"

I blurted out an emphatic yes. *I wanted Leo so badly that I took fertility drugs to get pregnant, you idiot. How could you ask such a blatantly inappropriate question and how could my answer directly relate to finding a remedy that would make Leo less weepy?* His question rendered me incapable of speech.

He prescribed Calcarea Carbonica, a natural "cure" for people who suffer from obsessive behavior, anxiety, and fear of failure. *Was this for me?* I never called him again for my follow-up appointment. But I still bought the remedy. It didn't work (not even for me).

Elimination Diet

I moved to pursue the next alternative therapy—a menu free of gluten, a protein found in flour; and casein, a protein in dairy products. Some people believe these proteins are incompletely digested and produce opioid-like substances that leak through tiny holes in the intestinal lining, which triggers an allergic reaction that causes or worsens autism. This is called "leaky gut syndrome." It sounded gross but believing in a leaky gut had a big following among those who also believed that autism is a disorder caused by a malfunction of the body's immune system. Believers contend that removing food substances that cause opioid proteins, namely sources of gluten and casein, would ameliorate the symptoms of autism and, in some cases, offer a cure. The diet was hard to follow because gluten can be found in so many substances, including soy sauce and the coatings of pills used for medicine. Eliminating dairy is almost as difficult.

This theory was on the outer boundary of what I was willing to believe. I sided with the medical community in believing that autism was primarily a genetic disorder affecting the central nervous system. I pursued testing Leo's tolerance for gluten and casein for general health reasons and to rule out other medical conditions, such as celiac disease, an obscure but lifelong intestinal disorder that prevents nutrients from being absorbed. Celiac disease is also treated through the elimination of wheat and dairy. To my relief, all of the tests for intolerance to gluten and casein came back negative, and I checked this diet off my list.

Other moms and experts bombarded me with advice about what else I should try. The Feingold diet. Neurofeedback. Vision therapy. Horseback riding therapy.

Dr. Feingold claims that there is a link between hyperactivity in children and the consumption of artificial colors and flavors, and foods high in salicylates, such as raisins, strawberries, and orange juice. I just could not imagine abandoning familiar foods in favor of organic and chemical-free food products. That would be too much work when there wasn't enough scientific evidence to back the claims. I eliminated the Feingold protocol.

Neurofeedback

My last-resort therapy was neurofeedback, a controversial attention-training and emotional regulation treatment for children with a variety of mental health disorders, chiefly attention deficit hyperactivity disorder (ADHD). But the technique, which surfaced in the 1970s to treat stress and migraines, had not won acceptance in the medical community to treat ADHD and other forms of mental illness. My sisters-in-law, both with doctorates in psychology who

had received training in neurofeedback, raved about it and supported me.

I was convinced that neurofeedback would help Leo gain greater control over his emotions. Underlying my compulsion to help Leo was a wish to perfect Leo until his progress matched my idea of what he'd be like if he were normal, like Lucas. Lucas, a hunk of a seven-year-old, excelled at sports and thrived socially among his peers. While I didn't expect Leo to become a social butterfly, I had hoped he'd make friends and play on a soccer team.

In neurofeedback, therapists put sensors on the scalp and wire them to a computer. The sensors measure and display a child's brainwaves on a computer screen. Brainwave activity is divided into frequencies that reflect different brain states: alert and focused, or drowsy and inattentive. The goal: Teach children with attention problems to control—and retrain—their brainwaves. To accomplish this, the child sits in a big, cushy chair and watches a computer monitor that displays either a video game or a movie. Through mind control (changing brainwave frequency), the child can control the screen action—get the characters in a video game to move, or play the movie. When brainwaves leave an optimal state, the child receives negative feedback; the movie ends or the game action stops.

I found a psychologist close to home, in an old apartment building. He recommended 30 one-hour sessions, costing $135 a session, which had to be paid on the spot. A quick calculation put the cost at about $4,800. He doubted that our health insurer would cover the expense. "Send me a receipt," I said.

I didn't tell him Leo's diagnosis out of fear that he'd look at Leo differently and judge his abilities based on just the word "autism." I can't say I was impressed with his demeanor, especially after he handed me a book on reactive attachment disorder (RAD), a poorly understood mental disorder that is marked by a child's inability to bond, leading to violent, bizarre behavior. He said it was the best

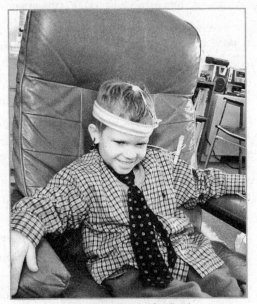

Leo receives neurofeedback.

book he'd ever read. Was he implying that my child was a RAD kid? Leo could form loving relationships, though he did throw temper tantrums. I got confused, and my emotions prevailed. I started treatments for Leo.

For his first session in early January, Leo sat in a leather chair that dwarfed his small frame. The doctor hooked up the electrodes, holding them in place with a red elastic headband and bobby pins. "What's your favorite video?" he said, while displaying his offerings. Leo picked the movie *Babe*, a story of a naïve talking piglet. Leo and I watched Babe almost befriend Rex, the head dog on the farm, before the screen went black. Leo's mental state had left the desired "zone," and hence, the movie stopped. When his brainwaves returned to the appropriate frequency, the movie would resume.

I later talked to my sisters-in-law about how boring it seemed,

and they said to ask the pscyhologist about using video games. I did. His system didn't work with video games. My sisters-in-law asked if they could talk to him. I authorized the doctor to discuss Leo's case. They emailed him a few times, but he never responded.

When I got the receipt, it had the wrong insurance codes, and I asked him to redo it, but he never did. We went for about two months paying $270 a week, without even an opportunity to file for reimbursement with our insurance company. Soon thereafter, I stopped neurofeedback. It made no difference in Leo's behavior.

◄ PRACTICAL ADVICE ►

Separating Legitimate Treatments from Snake Oil

Alternative treatments sink into a quagmire of controversy. There are multiple schools of thought and strong passions on the effectiveness of these therapies, which researchers call pseudo- and voodoo science because providers give the impression that they use scientific methods to prove their claims, but their results cannot be replicated. Treatments in this category include auditory integration training, neurofeedback, nutritional supplements, and special diets.

After that, the efficacy of treatments continues to spiral downward. Facilitated communication, holding therapy, rapid prompting, and even marijuana brownies fall into the category of bogus treatments. The Web is fertile ground for these bogus treatments. You're likely to come across facilities that pitch themselves online as "autism repair institutes" that offer "free samples" in the form of videos showing a child often acting wildly before treatment. You, the viewer, have no information about the child and whether he ever received an autism diagnosis. All you're shown is the child calmly playing imaginatively and making eye contact with a caregiver after a few months of treatment. There is no sound.

Such vivid and uplifting video testimonials are seductive. They lead parents to believe that their child can emerge out of her "frightening world" and become warmly engaged and focused for learning. But if you ask their backers to prove their claims, they'll likely say that they lack research dollars to test their method, or the method cannot be tested at all.

Many of these treatments develop a following after they are popularized by what later proves to be a misguided hypothesis or a poorly designed research study. For example, medical experts searched for emotional causes of autism after the disorder was named in the 1940s. This led to the "refrigerator mother" theory, which blamed autism on an unloving mother.

During this theory's heyday, clinicians treated children with psychoanalysis, which was based on Sigmund Freud's theory that early childhood experiences lay at the root of unhealthy brain development. The underlying belief considered autism a mental illness as opposed to a developmental disability.

Rigorous research later disproved this theory, but not until after world-famous Chicago psychologist Bruno Bettelheim promoted

▶ **FAST FACT**

While some alternative treatments may be generally benign in some respects, that doesn't mean they don't cause indirect harm in other ways to you and your child. Alternative therapies typically cost thousands of dollars, often require upfront payment, and are unlikely to be covered by your health insurance plan. They also involve rigorous treatment and time demands, which can leave you feeling guilty if you don't adhere to them. For example, eliminating foods when there is no distinct disease sets a child up for psychological and social stress because it teaches the child to view foods as threatening to his health and to eat differently in the company of others. Special diets are also difficult to maintain and risk lowering your child's caloric intake if he refuses the new food.

it. Bettelheim practiced and advocated "parentectomy," which involved removing children from their parents for a long time. Bettelheim's approach to treating autism through psychoanalysis led to claims of child abuse against him. The accusations were as spectacular as his suicide in 1990.

In the 1970s, the treatment that inspired hope in parents but did not survive scientific scrutiny was facilitated communication, a technique some call "Ouija board communication," because another person, or facilitator, supports a child's hand or elbow on a keyboard and types out messages the child is thinking. There are other forms of facilitated communication. Several controlled studies refuted this technique, and several academic societies, such as the American Academy of Pediatrics and the American Psychological Association, have issued policy statements against its use. Remarkably, to this day, Syracuse University maintains the Facilitated Communication Institute.

Ten years later, another fad treatment, Nystatin, an antifungal medicine used to treat women with yeast infections, emerged. Supporters implicated candida, a type of yeast that occurs naturally in everyone but which can grow out of control under the right conditions, as the cause of autism when some children who'd had yeast infections later developed symptoms of autism. The theory rested on studies showing that candida produced toxins and disrupted

▶ **INFORM YOURSELF** ————————————————————————

To separate good science from bad science, get *Life Journey Through Autism: A Parent's Guide to Research*, published by the Organization for Autism Research:* Learn how to interpret and understand autism research studies with this free guide. It also offers resources to locate the latest research findings in the field.

* www.researchautism.org/resources/reading/index.asp

animals' immune systems, possibly damaging their brains. If an overgrowth of candida could weaken the immune system in animals, then why wouldn't that be the case with children with yeast infections? Reseachers later dismissed this theory for lack of evidence. Nonetheless, antifungal medications, such as Nystatin, endure as a treatment for autism.

Nystatin is considered a biological treatment because it goes into the body. Other biological and alternative treatments include nutritional supplements, including vitamin B6 with magnesium and cod liver oil; elimination diets; secretin, an intestinal hormone; and chelation, a procedure to remove heavy metals from the body. Chelation is a valid treatment for removing lead, but it is not an accepted medical practice for treating autism. Its use is based on the disproved theory that mercury in thimerosal, a preservative used in the triple jab to prevent measles, mumps, and rubella (MMR), causes autism. If the mercury is removed from the body, then the symptoms of autism will go away.

Although a comprehensive report sponsored by the National Institutes of Health and the Centers for Disease Control and Prevention found no association between autism and thimerosal in vaccines, the topic continues to ignite visceral reactions from parents

▶ **FAST FACT** ────────────────────────────

The National Standards Project* brings together leading experts in autism treatment with the goal of evaluating treatment literature and establishing best practices for treating children and young adults on the autism spectrum. This panel, which is primarily composed of behaviorists, plans to establish and ratify a set of evidence-based guidelines in the areas of educational practices and procedures and treatment intervention. The National Autism Center is spearheading the project.

* www.nationalautismcenter.org

still convinced that a link between them exists and is the reason their children developed autism. Some even go so far as to accuse the federal government of a cover-up to protect vaccine manufacturers from lawsuits. *The Schafer Autism Report,** a fee-based electronic news clipping service on everything related to autism, follows the debate.

Nonbiological treatments consist of therapies that aren't digested. They include auditory integration training, which supposedly retrains the ear to listen better; neurofeedback, which supposedly retrains the brain to focus more; facilitated communication; and others. According to the American Academy of Pediatrics, 50 percent or more of families of children with autism spectrum disorders turn to both traditional and alternative treatments, sometimes even before a diagnosis is confirmed,[11] despite the American Medical Association's position that "there is little evidence to confirm the safety or efficacy of most alternative therapies."

In selecting a treatment for your child, consult with your intervention team or other professional whom you trust. But beware of their biases. Ask them about their philosophies toward treatments, where they earned their degree, and if they're certified in a particular method.

Different disciplines of practice have their own dispositions. For example, doctors schooled in biomedical treatments are likely to recommend treatment options that would address digestive disorders and metabolic problems as opposed to doctors certified in behavior analysis.

By educating yourself, you can spend less time guessing and more time making an informed decision about your child's treatment.

* www.sarnet.org

A Word on Medicating Your Child

To some parents, medication is often seen as a last resort and creates friction in a relationship when one parent wants to medicate and the other does not. The decision to medicate depends on so many factors, which are beyond the scope of this book. What's important to understand is that there are no medications that will make your child more social or more verbally articulate.

But sometimes medications can help control problem behaviors, such as aggression, irritability, anxiety, unstable moods, and hyperactivity. Even then, children's responses to them will differ, often widely. While one child's behavior might improve on a certain medication, that same medication may exacerbate an unwanted behavior in another child.

Many parents medicate their children to diffuse an explosive character, anxiety, and anxiousness, which are common traits of children with autism spectrum disorders. The definition given by Dr. Timothy E. Wilens, in his book *Straight Talk About Psychiatric Medications for Kids*, describes poor self-regulation as "an excessive response to a typical environmental stimulus or stressor, such as a child's extreme anger at normal parental requests." This behavior is called "mood reactivity."

Without understanding the root cause of problem behaviors, many experts discourage medication to control them. The first step then is to identify triggers that create uncomfortable, stressful, or explosive situations for a child and develop a support plan to lessen the behaviors. This process is called a functional behavioral assessment (FBA) and typically involves a psychologist who gathers information from parents and/or teachers. Sometimes a psychologist or a certified behavior analyst will directly observe your child, but finding a psychologist who will come to your home or visit your child's school is often difficult. The information is then reviewed and a behavioral support plan is developed and implemented with guidance from the psychologist.

For example, if your child gets upset when you run out of chicken nuggets, you might need to model appropriate language by saying "no big deal" to help your child interpret, or "grade," the disappointment. Or if you know a particular situation, say, a transition or request, is likely to upset your child, you might begin with the words: "I know you're not going to like this, but . . ." Sometimes, simple and basic tricks can help prepare your child for "the message" you are about to deliver. These techniques don't always work and they wear out when they do, but they are worth trying. Just remember to be consistent with the approaches outlined in your child's FBA.

Before starting any medication, it is important to rule out other medical factors as the cause of a problem behavior. Work with your pediatrician to identify a licensed child psychiatrist or medical doctor who specializes in pharmacology to treat mental health and emotional disorders if you're interested in exploring medications, such as Risperdal, which has been approved by the U.S. Food and Drug Administration to treat some behavioral symptoms associated with autism. Remember, medications are not a panacea and they're not necessarily lifelong, but they might help alleviate some behavioral problems so that your child is more ready and available to learn. There is no single recommended age for starting medication.

Inform Yourself

THE "DIET": SUCCESSFUL FOR SOME

Should you try "the diet"?

The diet refers to a biomedical intervention that calls for eliminating certain foods—chiefly sources of wheat and dairy—that anecdotal evidence shows induce or worsen the symptoms of autism. Biomedical interventions seek to change a child's physiology. Medication is another biomedical intervention; as is chelation therapy, gold salts, and nutritional supplements.

The main theory behind the diet: When wheat and dairy products are digested, enzymes in the intestines break them down into proteins consisting of long chains of amino acids. However, if the enzymes don't break down all of the proteins, short chains of amino acids, known as peptides, will result. These peptides are undigested chunks of proteins. While most of the peptides will pass through the urine, some will permeate the intestinal lining, flow into the bloodstream, and react with opioid receptors in the brain, which slows down the brain like an opiate drug, such as morphine. According to the theory, this reaction can affect behavior and impair cognition and communication (Great Plains Laboratory offers a Gluten/Casein Peptide Test).*

The offending protein in dairy is called casein, which is found in cheese, milk, and yogurt, and the protein in wheat and other grains, such as barley and rye, is gluten. Thus, the name Gluten-Free/Casein-Free, or GF/CF, diet. Other less obvious sources: casein is used as a binder in canned tuna fish, and envelope glue may be made from wheat. Some parents ask if eggs are a source of dairy. Even though both are found in the same refrigerated section of your grocery store, the answer is no.

Eliminating these foods forms the foundation for the basic GF/CF diet, but there is no definitive proof that it works. "There are a number of studies, but they are easy to criticize, because it is almost impossible to get a homogeneous group of autistic kids," said nutrition and autism expert Kelly Dorfman. "Nobody likes the stupid diet, but it works in about one-third of the kids and in a way that nothing else does if peptides are the problem."

If understanding studies on this topic boggles your mind, I

* www.greatplainslaboratory.com

recommend reading *Life Journey Through Autism: A Parent's Guide to Research*, published by the Organization of Autism Research.* This guide will help you understand what makes a good study versus one that blurs the facts to emphasize the point proffered by the researchers who conducted the study.

The goal, however, is not to make the diet unnecessarily restrictive.

The explanation of how a GF/CF diet works is more complicated when framed in scientific terms. Both the Autism Research Institute† and the Autism Network for Dietary Intervention (ANDI)‡ offer abundant resources for learning more. The ANDI site has an excellent FAQ on dietary interventions, as well as links to studies on such interventions. The site stresses that there is no one "protocol" for intervention and encourages parents to understand the ramifications and potential benefits of this intervention. Many parents follow the DAN! (Defeat Autism Now!) dietary protocol, which is the cornerstone of DAN! approach.

Of all the alternatives therapies, the GF/CF diet is the one to try, said Dr. Temple Grandin, one of the most successful adults with autism, author, and designer of humane livestock facilities. In her experience, she said children with regressive autism, meaning they develop normally for about two years and then begin to lose skills, are most likely to respond. She says she's seen the diet work for about one out of five children who try it. At a minimum, Dr. Grandin recommends trying the diet for one month. At a maximum, three months. She also recommends eliminating corn, soy, and sugar and adding calcium supplements when milk is removed from a child's diet. Some experts say that if you can't pronounce the ingredient on the label, or there are too many ingredients, you should put the item back on the shelf.

* www.researchautism.org/resources/parents%20guide.pdf
† www.autism.com
‡ www.autismndi.com

Child psychologist Dr. Serena Wieder advises families to do what "makes sense" but don't get stuck on dietary interventions at the expense of developing a comprehensive intervention plan that would include other treatments. Just as with any child, she said it is important to rule out allergies, food sensitivities or gut issues. "These would distress anyone but can be especially stressful for children with developmental disorders," she said.

SOME BUDGETWISE ALTERNATIVE PRACTICES

Don't overlook your child's sensory problems, which often accompany an autism diagnosis but are not part of the diagnostic criteria. A child with autism can overreact to fluorescent lights, loud noises, a hug or something sticky. Dr. Temple Grandin, author of *Thinking in Pictures* and self-proclaimed autistic, says there are some low-cost solutions to help with a kid's sensory problems. Dr. Grandin acknowledges that there's no scientific proof behind them, but since they cost so little and won't do any direct harm, she says they're worth trying. Try sunglasses if fluorescent lights seem to be a problem. A child with autism may see the flicker of fluorescent lights, and sunglasses may diffuse the flicker so that a child can tolerate trips to a grocery store or shopping mall, where fluorescent lights are common. Pick a pale shade because dark shades are hard to read through, and try on several colors. "When you find the right color, the lights will stop flickering for some children," she said. "Nobody knows how it works." A weighted vest may help calm an overactive child. Just don't let your child wear it all day, she said. She recommends twenty minutes on and twenty minutes off. Velvasoft* is a source of weighted clothing and blankets for children. Dr. Grandin also said exercise is especially important for children on the spectrum.

* www.world-net.net/home/mwsales/index.html

EIGHT

▶ ▶ ▶ **Educating Your Child:
Getting It Right**

I passed several blocks of red brick row houses before I saw the massive school towering over the neighborhood, covering an entire city block. I knew that was Barnard Elementary School in Northwest DC. It had recently been rebuilt, replacing crumbling walls and missing windows with all the modern amenities, including high ceilings, skylights, and sensors in the rooms that turned the lights on and off.

Inside, I found my way to the principal's office, passing brightly painted walls and a cool stretch of floor tiles. The principal led me to the special education class and introduced me to Mrs. Brooks, the teacher.

I sat at a table near the back of the room while Mrs. Brooks resumed reading a story about a chicken and her baby chick. "Cock-a-doodle-doo," she crowed, prompting the children to imitate her. Of the eleven children, five could participate. The children, from four to eight years old, had myriad disabilities, including autism, mental retardation, and cerebral palsy. When Mrs. Brooks finished the story, she asked the higher-functioning children to write the title of the book, draw their favorite part of the story, and write a sentence about it.

"The little ones can color," she told three aides, each dedicated to a child. A male aide handed out paper with outlines of different shapes and instructed the children to color them red. A small boy could not hold a crayon, and his personal aide helped him position the crayon between his fingers. Another aide asked a nonverbal girl whether she was right- or left-handed.

I thought I recognized the twin girls who had been in the Lafayette program the previous summer. Both had cerebral palsy and mental retardation. One of the girls, held upright in a four-wheel walker, propelled herself across the floor and reached out for the Venetian blinds. Another aide, standing near the blinds, threw a small gym mat in front of the blinds to block her path. The girl, perhaps five years old, bleated. The aide handed her a cracker. It pacified her.

The girl then flung herself to the other side of the room, maneuvering to reach a set of metal file cabinets. She picked up a stick of some sort and beat on them. The air echoed with a rat-a-tat-tat.

"She's probably going to grow up to be a drummer," the aide said, breaking out into a laugh and scanning the room to see whether the other aides would laugh with him. They didn't.

The aide's behavior shocked me. He appeared to have had no training on challenging behaviors and no idea how to manage them. It was inappropriate for him to joke about her actions, especially in front of me, a stranger. If he had been properly trained, he would have known to focus his attention on the girl by saying her name first and then kneeling down to speak to her face to face. He should have redirected her in clear and simple language. I didn't see any positive behavior reinforced, not even when the children colored. Just a simple "Look at what you've colored. Pretty picture!" would have been enough to bring a smile to one of their faces. I hadn't expected a program worse than the special education classroom at Lafayette Elementary School, which I had observed the previous year, and hid my disgust.

As Mrs. Brooks assisted the children with their assignment, a child interrupted her. "It's my turn to talk," Mrs. Brooks said. "That means you listen. If you don't know what to do, you're not going to turn in good paper."

Ten minutes later, the younger children were still coloring shapes. Mrs. Brooks instructed the aides to pass out blank pieces of paper. She kept the little kids coloring. An older girl with mental retardation folded her paper in half. She folded the paper again and again, ignoring the instructions to draw. "We don't fold paper," the aide said. "We color. We draw on it, but we don't fold paper."

I couldn't believe what he was saying. It was so upsetting. The girl could learn something from folding paper—fine motor skills—and the point was that she had the skills to fold paper, and she was showing initiative and creativity. Moments later, another aide scolded a boy with autism for bringing in a toy action figure. "I told you not to bring in toys," he said. "You're not doing your work. I'll put you in a time-out if you play with toys all day." The boy cowered in his chair and hid his head between his arms. The aide turned. I kept taking notes. The girl was folding paper again. "I told you not to fold the paper. It's not funny. It's not a joke." The girl almost cried.

After forty-five minutes, I had seen enough. I could not send Leo there.

When Special Education Works

Granted, my experience with the District of Columbia public school system was a travesty of errors and is not meant to characterize the state of special education across the nation. In Syracuse, our experience with the special education system was positive. We worked in the spirit of the law, as a team, and felt Leo received the services necessary to acquire skills defined in his intervention plan. Our family also received supports—a social worker and respite care, which provided money to reimburse a babysitter and get a break from being a full-time caregiver. All was paid for by the government, as it should be, in order to educate all children.

The Syracuse city school system worked, I believe, because it contracted with private special ed schools, such as Jowonio, the school my son attended, rather than force children into low- and no-quality programs because that's all it could manage to offer. If more school systems followed that model, there would be less fighting between schools and parents.

Before we moved to DC, I had searched for a school that replicated Jowonio's inclusion model, and though choices were limited, St. Columba's Nursery School rose to the top of my list. St. Columba's wasn't a special ed school like Jowonio, but it openly accepted children with special needs and nourished the sensory needs of children like my son, who overreacted to loud noises by crying and had unwarranted temper outbursts.

I first observed St. Columba's in November 2001, when Leo had been in early intervention for less than six months. The director, Karen Strimple, agreed to give David and me a tour even though there were no openings midyear when we planned to move from Syracuse. Recess was in progress when we arrived. David stayed on the playground with Lucas and Leo while Karen showed me the classrooms. I flipped back the mental notes I had made while still in Syracuse visiting some other preschools that my social worker had shown me in preparation for my visit. She told me what to look for: pictures that showed each routine of the day, designated corners for reading books, art and pretend play, a sensory table filled with sand or some other substance, such as rice or water, and sunlight to fill the room. St. Columba's had all these qualities and more, especially the playground.

On one end of the playground there stood a low hedge of bushes that hid a small trail, and down a slope grew tall hemlocks with low-lying branches that the children were allowed to climb. Directly through the wrought-iron gate, laughter spilled out of the window of a small playhouse as four little boys reenacted the story of the three little pigs. Directly in front lay a big sandbox, with children, in plastic hard hats, digging holes. Swings, slides, and climbing structures were everywhere. The teachers stood back and let the children explore but rushed in if a child struggled with negotiating the leadership of play or some other social interaction. I watched and absorbed.

Karen had worked at the school for nearly thirty years. She guided her children to learn and explore their senses and paid attention to their development, bringing in therapists at the start of every school year to screen the children for developmental delays. If a problem was identified, Karen pressed parents to intervene. Throughout the year, therapists routinely visited the school to provide therapy to children if their parents requested it.

I believe Leo got in because we assured Karen that we didn't expect St. Columba's to "fix" Leo and that we would involve ourselves with his needs, which, in our case, meant finding and paying for a one-to-one aide. Even with twelve children in a class and two teachers, a child with special needs will require more attention, and teachers struggle with providing that attention while attending to the other children. Having an aide to help Leo facilitate social interactions or calm him when he became upset relieved the tension between these competing interests.

While DC school officials had paid the tuition of children with IEPs (Individualized Education Programs) at St. Colomba's in previous years, it did not have a contract with the school to serve them. It also wasn't a given that the system would recommend and then pay for a placement at St. Columba's. In my case, school officials ignored Leo's intervention plan from Syracuse that called for inclusion and instead sought to place him in a special ed classroom at a public elementary school—a decision that forced my husband and me to take legal action. Since school officials can't force parents to send their child to the school it recommends (it can only refuse to pay for it), we sent Leo to St. Columba's.

◄ PRACTICAL ADVICE ►

On a special needs online bulletin board, a mother wrote:

> But . . . we have MONEY! We could hire a one-on-one therapist or a babysitter with special needs training, but my husband and I really want our son to be with typically developing preschoolers for socialization and peer learning. Any suggestions? Is there such a thing as a pricey, integrated exceptional-needs preschool?
>
> Signed, Will Pay for the Right Preschool

Finding the right school setting is absolutely worth obsessing about and often goes beyond an act of love to an act of desperation. Is there, as this mother asks, such a thing as "a pricey, integrated exceptional-needs preschool"? On the flip side, you also may ask, "Is there a traditional special education program?"

The answer to both questions is "yes." But such schools may not exist in your neighborhood or neighboring counties. You may have to search the entire nation to find an effective educational program for your child.

That, of course, is an extreme step, but some parents dramatically alter their lives to help their child. In the race against time to set your child on a developmental path that will lead to independent living, the urgency is almost primal.

Before you hunt elsewhere, explore the options in your area. Remember, you're not choosing a school because its graduates attended a school in the Ivy League; you're selecting an educational program that has qualified and caring teachers who can help your child learn skills he or she needs to participate as fully in life as possible.

There are four steps to the process:

▶ Define your child's needs.

▶ Compare educational programs.

▶ Evaluate the skill set of teachers.

▶ Pick the right program.

Often the best advice you can get about choosing the right program will come from other parents who've been there. So, start networking. Your church, synagogue, or faith-based group is a natural first step. Another is to find a local chapter of the Autism Society of America* and attend a support group. These parent-led groups offer a healthy source of information about school districts and educational programs.

Define Your Child's Needs

But before you adopt their advice, step back and answer some hard questions: What does your child need?

If your child cannot attend to a task, will not express needs, or resists adult-directed activities, placing him in an environment with nondisabled children may not be wise at this point in his development. In this case, consider a more specialized environment that

* www.autism-society.org

teaches self-help skills and provides more one-on-one or small-group instruction.

If, on the other hand, your child can sometimes use language appropriately and displays rudimentary social skills, you wouldn't want to subject her to a specialized class where the teacher, for example, might prompt the children to say "meow" in a lesson about cats when she could benefit from a higher-level interpretation.

For the context of this explanation, let's assume your child will go through the IEP or IFSP process, rather than bypass the Individuals with Disabilities Education Act, the federal special education law that is designed to educate all children with disabilities.

IEP stands for Individualized Education Program, and IFSP means Individualized Family Service Plan. Your child's age will determine the plan. As a general rule, children under three will fall under your community's early intervention office, which will write an IFSP, while an IEP covers children from age three through adulthood, defined as age twenty-one. Your local school district, specifically your neighborhood school, will meet with you to develop an IEP.

The heart of each plan identifies skills that will be most useful for your child to learn in the next six months to a year. An IEP, however, outlines a child's education and places more emphasis on academic achievement than an IFSP, which describes desired "outcomes," called goals in IEP parlance, and lists early intervention services needed to achieve them. These services are delivered in environments where very young children and their families spend time, such as the home or in child care. Both are legal documents and the single most critical documents that determine your child's services.

A few more key points: Under an IEP, your child is entitled to a "free and appropriate education," called a FAPE. The "free" part should be easy to understand: The law provides a funding mechanism to pay for your child's special education services. Understanding what "appropriate" means in the context of the law is more difficult to grasp. That's because the law does not define this term, and its meaning has been left up to courts. As imprecise as this reads, an educational program is considered appropriate if it is "sufficient to confer some educational benefit," as measured through both educational and social progress.[12] Put plainly, don't expect a specific level of achievement or even a regular high school diploma for your child.

Family members, your child's therapists, child-care teachers, and your early intervention service coordinator will work as a team to develop and implement your IFSP. A similar process occurs with the development of an IEP. Other members of an IEP team would include school system officials, teachers, and program specialists. During this process, you may not feel that representatives from early intervention, or the school district, are "on your side." The educational programs offered may boil down to a "take it or leave it" choice. If you dispute a placement, which is your right, the law specifies how to resolve the dispute through mediation; due process, which is like an administrative hearing; or a court case, which is the most costly alternative.

Important note: Don't ever say you want a "better" placement. Stick to the legal jargon by saying you don't think the placement is "appropriate." Too often parents unwittingly sabotage their own case by apologetically explaining to the IEP team that they are only doing what they think is "best" for their child, that they want to "maximize" the gains. Another thing that happens with conniving school districts is that the IEP team chair will comment to the parents that if he were in their shoes he'd also to want what was best for his child, with the caveat that the law doesn't provide for a best education or one that "maximizes" a child's potential. Upon hearing this, the parents smile, nod in agreement, feel heard and understood, and the meeting continues. Later, if a dispute arises, the school district representative testifies that that the parents knew what they wanted was best for their child, while they also acknowl-edged that the school's program was appropriate. This sets up parents for losing their case.

If you pooh-pooh the system and turn your back, you put your-self in a tricky spot because you'll now be responsible for paying for your child's education and other services, such as speech and occupational therapy. You may opt for that, but think of the long-term consequences. Such a drastic step may be unhealthy for your finances and marriage. It's better to understand the rules and hire an expert to ensure they're followed.

One type of expert to consider is an educational advocate, gen-erally a person with a master's in special education. The Internet, however, offers troves of information about parent advocacy and free legal services, which are difficult to qualify for. Nonetheless, take advantage of these resources with a word of caution: Pay attention to the source of the material because outdated informa-tion and misinformation abounds on the Internet. In 2004, the fed-eral law changed, and new rules became effective in 2005.

Compare Educational Options

Broadly speaking, your options range from inclusion in a regular school to a home-based program. In between are a selection of spe-cial education programs, from the traditional special education school to a special ed classroom in a regular school.

One of the big pluses of inclusion programs is that disabled chil-dren are allowed to learn alongside their nondisabled peers. Being given an opportunity to observe and imitate peers helps children with disabilities develop social interaction skills.

Full inclusion involves educating all children in regular class-rooms all the time, regardless of the degree or severity of a disabil-ity. Although schools are becoming more inclusive, inclusion is not a right, and it is not written into the federal law. Instead, the law refers to Least Restrictive Environment (LRE), yet another legal term that is akin to a "mainstreaming" policy. LRE requires school districts to place students into a regular classroom setting "to the maximum extent possible," another of those legal terms open to interpretation. If your child could benefit from LRE, that needs to be written into the plan.

A disadvantage of inclusion programs is the high ratio of teachers to students. In a special ed classroom, the ratio might be as low as one teacher for every two students, while a regular classroom may have twenty-five kids with one teacher and an assistant, neither of whom is likely to be trained in the needs of disabled children. A special ed classroom in a regular school, however, has a more favorable ratio—ten to twelve students per one teacher and two aides.

There is no federal policy that sets student-teacher ratios, nor does anything require states to set them. The issue is left up to states entirely.

Evaluate Teachers' Skills

Special ed teachers are required to have a master's degree and be certified in the state they teach. Their more advanced education trains them to teach and to understand and tolerate the behaviors of students with disabilities. But to teach language and other skills, they may not be trained in intensive behavioral intervention (IBI), which is how many experts refer to applied behavior analysis (ABA).

In case you cannot locate qualified teachers, the reality of your situation may be to create a home-based program. A home-based program, consisting of twenty-five to forty hours per week, will require your full-time attention to manage effectively. You'll need to find a consultant, such as a psychologist with special training; and you'll have to recruit, train, schedule, and manage therapists, often students with little or no experience in IBI. Turnover is high.

Pick the Right Program

Your team has defined your child's needs. You've compared educational programs and reviewed the teaching skills of the instructional staff. Of all the programs you've observed, is there a direct match for the learning needs of your child? If there is, push for it. If there isn't, you have two options. You can either create your own unique program or take a hybrid approach that includes some

▶ **FAST FACT**

WAIT LIST TIPS. Services exist to help parents create an in-home program. But you might be placed on a long waiting list because the service has too few therapists or supervisors. If that happens, here are three tips to jump-start your program.

Therapist shortage. Ask if any supervisors are available. Tell the provider that you'd be willing to find your own therapists if the provider will staff your in-home program with one of its supervisors.

Supervisor shortage. Ask for an experienced therapist to work with your child while you continue your search for a supervisor. Ideally, find a psychologist trained in behavior modification or is a Board Certified Behavior Analyst or Board Certified Associate Behavior Analyst. See "How to Find and Train Student Therapists," pages 127–29.

Parent workshops. If you strike out on both fronts—no therapists or supervisors available—ask if the provider holds parent-training workshops to learn basic skills, or if the provider knows of a group that does.

Assessing your child before an in-home program begins is essential. The assessment will determine the skills she needs to learn.

school system services and others that you find outside the system. Both are doable but difficult to establish and maintain. In-home programs, for example, take time to set up and the high cost—more than $1,000 a month, depending on the hourly rate of therapists— is not always covered by insurance or your school district. Recruiting and training therapists is another obstacle, especially if you don't live near a university.

As you decide, center on this question: Will my child be able to learn in this setting? Under ideal circumstances, the learning environment will teach your child how to "generalize," which means to transfer knowledge from one situation to another. In other words, if your child recognizes the moon in a board book, will he be able to recognize the moon in the sky as the same object? Teaching children with autism to generalize what they see and learn across a variety of settings is critical since they do not acquire language spontaneously and naturally by observing and modeling the language of

▶ **INFORM YOURSELF** ————————————————————

Sources of specialized programs and schools. The Interdisciplinary Council on Developmental and Learning Disorders has compiled a list of programs and schools that embrace the DIR/Floortime model.* Another helpful site listing specialized day schools comes from the Help Group.† You also can search using the key phrase "ABA schools" (keep the quotes around the key phrase; it forces some search engines to search for the exact phrase). A model ABA program is the STARS (Strategic Teaching and Reinforcement Systems) School in Walnut Creek, California.‡ Easter Seals is the largest provider of inclusive child care in the United States, with more than ninety centers across the nation.§

* www.icdl.com/resources
† www.thehelpgroup.org/programs.htm
‡ www.behavioranalysts.com/Stars_school.html
§ www.easterseals.com/site/PageServer?pagename=ntl_child_development_centers

others. If you don't believe a particular setting will help your child to learn, look elsewhere.

Your decision should also involve the competency of the teachers. Can they teach critical skills? And is the learning environment conducive to acquiring new skills?

Once you select an educational program, involve yourself and monitor your child's progress. Check in with the teachers. Start an email discussion list that includes daily or weekly updates. Your child's needs will change, sometimes more rapidly than you might think. Be prepared to change your child's program as your child progresses.

NINE

▶ ▶ ▶ **Advocating for Your Child's Rights**

All the roles I had taken on as an adult—student, journalist, entrepreneur, wife, mother—had been by choice. Leo's diagnosis spun me around and forced the role of advocate upon me, a role I had not sought out and, in fact, had never considered. Until then I had been more or less what the French call *une femme de l'exterieur*, meaning a woman focused on the world outside the home. My mother was the nurse, the professional caregiver. Surely my emerging identity was built on the roles I had already mastered, and in reorienting myself to deal with Leo's challenges, I had varying degrees of confidence, perseverance, and intelligence on my side.

If starting to understand the nature of Leo's illness and deciding on the best treatments weren't complicated enough in Syracuse, Washington was another matter entirely. Reason might lead to the hope that we'd be better off in Washington—a wealthy region that attracts bright minds from across the nation to work in the government, its universities, think tanks, and hospitals. Surely it had better therapists and more treatment options. Syracuse is at best a second-tier city, being steadily pushed into the third tier with each passing year. What advantages could it truly be expected to have over the nation's capital?

As I was to learn painfully over the course of the next two years, in polite Syracuse all I had to do to receive the necessary services was to ask. In the District of Columbia, I had to be prepared to go to war. I would need to become good at it or risk failing at the role most important to me—being Leo's mom.

Learning the "System"

Like any parent seeking services under federal special education law, we went through the process of meeting with school officials, determining whether Leo was eligible, and then defining the type and amount of services necessary for him to see progress. Another part of the process was determining where he would go to school.

The choices were either special education, meaning Leo would be contained in a classroom with other children who had disabilities, or inclusion. Leo's Syracuse intervention plan called for inclusion.

When parents disagreed with the school system, Sandra Mailman, our lawyer, said parents could take advantage of a mechanism in the law that allowed them to dispute their child's placement in a legal proceeding, known as a due-process hearing. She said due process separated the parents who would fight back from those who would not. Those who fought back stood a good chance of winning, she said, which meant that they got reimbursed for what they had spent to provide their child with what the school system failed to do.

She said the school system operated within two constraints.

First, any program it recommended had to be "free and appropriate." The school system's greatest difficulty, however, was meeting the requirement to educate Leo in the least restrictive environment, or LRE. We had letters stating that it would be detrimental to Leo's progress to place him in a restrictive or special education program.

Our IEP Meeting

At our last meeting with the school district in May 2002, the room was packed again with school officials, though not as many as before. A month earlier, at our first meeting, I could not believe fifteen school officials showed up.

Again, the occupational therapist wanted to dismiss Leo from occupational therapy because when he fell in a therapy session, he was able to hold on to his baby blanket, which showed that he could do two things at once. He recommended OT consultation.

"What does that mean?" David said.

"In school it means you consult with all of his teachers so that they can teach Leo how to rip or cut colored paper and then glue it to sheets of paper," he said.

The therapist said occupational therapy goals had to produce skills necessary for "meaningful" academic success—using scissors, holding a pencil, writing. But I said Leo's occupational therapy needs were related to helping his brain and nervous system effectively process information so he could remain emotionally regulated when faced with demands or activities to perform. I felt this was much more important than ensuring that Leo could cut on the dotted line. I was so infuriated at the occupational therapist for dismissing Leo's occupational therapy needs that I checked his licensing credentials with the DC Health Professional Licensing Administration and found, to my surprise, that he was licensed.

David was able to get the occupational therapist to recant his belief that Leo only needed OT consultation. He referred back to Leo's evaluation reports and hammered away at him about Leo's deficits until he relented. We moved on to discuss placement.

"The team recommends placing Leo in Lafayette," said Dr. Hartman, principal of Lucas's elementary school.

"The program is so thoroughly and totally inadequate that I can't fathom how it is part of the same process," David said.

I straightened up in my chair, flushed with anger. "The teacher uses TV to teach language," I said.

"Obviously, we are in disagreement," Dr. Hartman said coolly. "The early childhood office gave its recommendation for placement. You can sign that you were present. You don't have to sign that you agree. Are there any other issues?"

Although I wasn't surprised at the placement recommendation, I couldn't believe school officials proceeded to write goals to fit their programs rather than to fit Leo. The goals of an intervention plan drive the placement, and since Lafayette was the only program the school system had, they justified placing Leo there without discussion.

David and I refused to sign his new intervention plan. No sane parent would send their child to a warehousing program that wasn't even good babysitting. The special ed students at Lafayette were contained in a long, narrow room with no windows and only one exit for emergencies. Sometimes, a security guard helped out when an aide was absent—a reasonable substitute since neither appeared to have had any training on working with students with special needs. Disobedient children stood in the corner.

Due Process: A Legal Recourse

Summer and fall flew by in a blur, and our due-process hearing was upon us. Our lawyer briefed us on the process and prepped us on our dress and demeanor, which amounted to don't speak unless you're spoken to, no flashy jewelry, and stick to the facts.

A hearing officer—someone who is typically a lawyer and independent of the school system—would conduct the hearing at the headquarters for the DC Office of Special Education. As in a courtroom trial, each side would present its case, offer witnesses, and submit evidence. It boiled down to a dispute over which placement—Lafayette or St. Columba's, the private inclusion nursery school we had found—was appropriate.

I could understand why the District wanted to serve more of its students with special needs in less costly District facilities. But since the District was light-years behind offering adequate programs, why were its administrators putting our family through this fight? Surely all the educational services that the school district offered to provide, including the cost of the Lafayette program as bad as it was, couldn't have totaled that much less than what we had shelled out for the services we had found ourselves. St. Columba's tuition amounted to $5,500 a year, a relatively measly sum compared to other private schools, and the District was using up many hours of manpower and the cost of legal counsel to argue with us.

Nonetheless, the hearing proceeded on time and on schedule. A Perry Mason–like drama this was not. Instead, it was a combination legal hearing and telephone conference call. Our lawyer was prepared to elicit favorable testimony and cross-examine witnesses, and the school system's lawyer looked as if he had just opened the file.

Sandra transformed the testimony of Dr. Cary Lion, the school psychologist, into a travesty by revealing that she knew little or nothing about Leo or the Lafayette program she was on record as recommending, which in turn raised doubts about what subject this expert was expert about. Sandra hammered away at what Dr. Lion exactly knew about Leo's current level of functioning.

"You haven't observed Leo at St. Columba's Nursery School, have you?" Sandra said.

"No," said Dr. Lion, who had been employed by the school district for fifteen years.

"Have you spoken to his parents since he's been there?"

"No, I have not," Dr. Lion said.

"Have you spoken to the educational consultant who was present at the meetings you attended to develop his IEP and determine his eligibility?" Sandra said.

"No, I have not."

"Did you observe him at the JumpStart program during the summer?"

"No, I did not," said Dr. Lion, her voice trailing to a near whisper.

"Do you know anything about the JumpStart program?"

"I am not familiar with the JumpStart program," Dr. Lion said.

"Did you talk to Dr. Terry?" said Sandra.

"No," said Dr. Lion.

"Did you talk to Dr. Volkmar?"

"No."

"Do you recall the discussion of placement?" said Sandra.

"I recall that Lafayette was proposed as a placement," Dr. Lion said.

Sandra continued her line of inquiry, asking Dr. Lion about whether she had reviewed the reports from Leo's therapeutic team that recommended an inclusion program. Dr. Lion could not remember what she had reviewed in preparation for Leo's IEP meeting.

Opposing counsel then called Dr. Hartman. Sandra instantly objected when Dr. Hartman attempted to testify about our case, a sensitive and confidential matter, by using a cell phone while on a walkathon with teachers, parents, and children in his school. Once on the school's line, she probed him to describe opportunities for Leo to engage with nondisabled children at Lafayette, but there wasn't much to say since the options, as we all knew by then, were limited to recess and lunch.

I admit that Dr. Hartman's poor performance gave me great satisfaction. He was a reasonably nice person, although perhaps a bit reserved. In my naiveté, I had thought that we could win him over with logic and research—facts. But when a man who holds both a master's and a doctorate in education administration and planning from an Ivy League school, who surely had ample time to consider the matter, said that *in his professional opinion* the school district offered adequate resources for my son to surmount his deficits, well, I never quite got over that. I felt sure that he knew it was wrong when he said it and was simply following the dictates of his employer. I can face ignorance, but I cannot stand a person who seems to be protecting the system at the expense of a child. Fortunately, the hearing officer was unconvinced by his testimony.

We received a decisive thumbs-up verdict and were awarded about $20,000. I'd like to think that we won because justice was on our side. Amid all that is horribly wrong and broken about special education and how our institutions address issues concerning children on the autism spectrum, there are some moments to savor when you feel the general consciousness of the world is slowly rising, and that people are starting to understand what these children need to be set on the proper course of development. The schools, the health insurance companies, the government—you fight all these institutions for some understanding and then, finally, for at least a moment, the angels are on your side.

◄ PRACTICAL ADVICE ►

Smart Starts in Special Education

Why struggle to understand the arcana of federal special education law? So that you know your rights and what direction to push the system to help your child.

Understanding the federal and state laws that govern special education will give you more leverage when disagreements arise. Even if you end up hiring professionals, the key decisions rest with you.

You are not obligated to accept a program simply because it exists or it is the only program offered by school officials. If you disagree with your child's intervention plan, the law provides several mechanisms for resolving disputes. A crucial concept worth repeating is that the law was written to guarantee equal opportunity, not a gold-plated education.

If you disagree with your school district, you cannot immediately leap into court with a lawsuit, however. You must try and work it out before you take your dispute to a higher level, which might be a trial-like procedure called a due-process hearing. It is held before an impartial hearing officer. At that hearing, you have the right to present evidence, cross-examine witnesses, be represented by an attorney, and obtain a written record of the hearing and a written decision.

A key revision of the newly updated law now requires that parents and school officials meet prior to a due-process hearing in an effort to resolve disputes. This meeting may take the form of a "resolution session," which is like an informal IEP meeting, or a mediation session, which utilizes an outside mediator appointed by the state to assist the parties in trying to resolve the dispute. This revision and others became effective July 1, 2005. If you lose due process, you can appeal the decision, and that will move your case into the state or federal court system.

Regardless of the legal venue, if you request a due-process hearing, you have the legal burden of proof that your child's plan will not provide a free and appropriate education. A 2005 U.S. Supreme Court decision (*Schaffer v. Weast*) placed the burden of proof on the party initiating and seeking relief, typically the parents.

If you are unsuccessful in a due-process hearing, you still have the option of providing the service or program you desire at your own expense. If you win, however, you will typically receive partial or full reimbursement for the attorney's fees you paid, but sometimes the school system may scale back the reimbursement if it believes they are excessive. As a result of a recent Supreme Court decision, parents may not recover the fees they pay for the assistance of outside experts who testify in due-process hearings.

A Sea of Acronyms, Rules, Definitions

Other important points: There is no one set of rules that interpret the federal law. Each state's special education law must comply with the basic standards of the federal law. However, states have some room to interpret certain details of the special education

▶ **FAST FACT**

The fact that your child may need intensive intervention does not mean federal special education law—the Individuals with Disabilities Education Act—is going to provide it, much less pay for it. As one special education lawyer put it: "IDEA is only meant to give you the serviceable Chevy, not the Cadillac of services"—meaning your child won't get the best services, just something that's adequate.

system that are not specifically addressed by the federal law, such as rules relating to class size. State law may provide more safeguards for children with disabilities than the federal law, but can never provide less protection.

The mumble-jumble of acronyms—FAPE, LRE, IEP, IFSP, FERPA—is daunting. Many terms have different meanings across states. But you need to speak and understand the language or risk being taken advantage of. Download *A Parent Primer on Special Education Acronyms, Abbreviations, and Definitions** from the Mountain Plains Regional Resource Center, a program funded by the U.S. Office of Special Education. This free pamphlet defines in plain English more than sixty commonly used special education terms.

Two other important terms to understand are Individual Family Service Plan (IFSP) and Individualized Education Program (IEP). These terms refer to your child's intervention plan, which is developed by a team that includes you. Your child will receive an IFSP if he or she is less than three years old. Children three and older receive an IEP. The law provides transition guidelines to move a child out of early intervention and into a school system program. This process typically begins six months before a child turns three.

Generally, both plans define your child's special education services, which must be based on your child's unique needs. They also specify any "related," or additional, services, including transportation to a school program, special therapy, and "assistive technology," which is any device, such as a keyboard, that helps a child with a disability enhance specific skill areas.

An IEP also describes your child's current level of academic achievement and functional performance, and includes goals, criteria for measuring the child's progress over the course of a year, and specifies the starting date, frequency, duration, and location where your child's services are to be delivered. An IFSP is similar but

---

* www.rrfcnetwork.org/content/view/181/56

includes family supports, such as counseling. An IEP can involve family supports, but it doesn't happen as much as with an IFSP. Services specified in an IFSP are generally delivered in a child's natural environment, such as a preschool or at home.

Unfortunately, some professionals in our educational system still view children with autistic spectrum disorders as a group, not as individuals. This stereotype has perpetuated the belief that children on the spectrum need the same intervention and will benefit from the same program. Sometimes professionals might want to segregate your child from children without disabilities, regardless of the severity of your child's diagnosis. Other times they might seek to place your child in an inclusive classroom with a one-on-one aide. What's important for you to know is that, if appropriate for your child's level of functioning, he or she has the right to learn in the same classroom as children without disabilities.

Whether that learning environment is appropriate for your child is a decision that your intervention team must answer. Remember, you are a team member, and you can invite other specialists who treat your child to join the team. Sometimes, however, your private specialists won't want to give up seeing other clients to attend your child's intervention plan meeting. Ask if they will write goals for you to present to the team or answer questions by telephone.

When to Hire Legal Experts

There are legal and medical experts you can hire, but their fees aren't necessarily covered by the federal law. Each plays a different role in the process.

The first step is to identify your child's needs and whether school district services are meeting them.

If they are not, you might want to start out hiring an educational advocate. Look for a person with a master's degree in special

► **INFORM YOURSELF** ───────────────────────────────

Don't let your next IEP meeting leave you emotionally charged, speech-less, or without adequate facts to support your position. Empower yourself with an online service designed especially for parents. It's called the Pop-Up IEP.* Each of the three pop-ups lists sixteen specific problematic comments school officials make, including, "We're not convinced that your child needs that," and "Your child's behaviors are disrupting the classroom." When you click on comments like that, you'll receive assertive yet courteous replies—and specific legal references.

Other excellent resources include the free e-learning class, *Partners in Education*.† This six-hour self-study course, created by Partners in Policymaking, walks you through the entire special education process. Another worth taking is *Making Your Case*.‡ You don't need to finish the courses in one sitting.

IFSPweb's§ graphical flow chart shows how the IFSP process works. Although the site is aimed at helping Nebraska parents and profession-als create better IFSPs, the self-paced tutorial offers insightful informa-tion on the process in general.

The National Center for Learning Disabilities** shows parents how best to engage policymakers and the media on learning disability issues. Read the *LD* Advocates Guide.†† Another starting point is Wrightslaw.‡‡ Its extensive library lists seminars on special education. It also reports on major court cases. LD Online§§ offers legal and advocacy tips from legal commentator Matt Cohen. A top resource in the "Parents" sec-tion is *Navigating the Special Education Process*. For book reviews, sign up for *Parenting Special Needs*.***

---

* (1) http://nclid.unco.edu/nclid/dhh (2) http://nclid.unco.edu/nclid/ssn/index.php
(3) http://nclid.unco.edu/nclid/bvi
† www.partnersinpolicymaking.com/education
‡ www.partnersinpolicymaking.com/makingyourcase
§ www.answers4families.org/ifspweb/process.html
** www.ncld.org
†† www.ncld.org/content/view/263/312
‡‡ www.wrightslaw.com
§§ www.ldonline.com
*** http://specialchildren.about.com/gi/pages/mmail.htm

The Bazelon Center for Mental Health Law,* a nonprofit organization that helps advocate for people with mental illness disabilities at the national level, offers extensive advocacy resources. It only takes individual cases that would have a national impact. Autism Speaks offers pro bono legal services to families, but you must meet its eligibility requirements, and your case must have reached the federal level. Visit the Federal Legal Appeal Project† to download an application.

* www.bazelon.org

† www.autismspeaks.org/howtocope/federal_legal_appeal.php

---

education. An advocate's role is to help identify problems and offer strategies for resolving disputes with your school district before a bigger conflict emerges. A special education attorney will handle your legal matters and advise you on the strength of your case if your relationship with the school district has landed you in due process. Your attorney also will know opposing counsel and the hearing examiners in due-process proceedings—two potentially big advantages.

Moreover, the law keeps changing. For example, new rules made significant changes in how schools determine whether a child has a specific learning disability, and the changes made for resolving disputes are another reason the help of a legal expert is advisable. And remember, once the law changes, states need to write rules to implement them. To keep up with that, visit the Early Intervention Family Alliance.‡ The "Projects" section explains these complicated rules in plain English and tells the pros and cons of what they mean.

You may want to consider other outside experts. If your child is having difficulty in school, you may seek a second opinion from a

‡ www.eifamilyalliance.org/index.html

health care professional. Outside evaluations are often valuable if you're concerned that the school is not doing its job.

Of course, you always have the right to bypass the system and obtain private or home-based services at your own expense, thereby avoiding some of the complexities and potential conflicts that arise in dealing with the school system. It is not recommended that you do this, even though the law allows for it. Unless you are financially independent, consider the high cost of special education services.

Do's and Don'ts

I'm not an attorney and am not qualified to give legal advice, but based on my experience and interviews with other parents and experts, here are some basics to keep in mind when entering the legal realm on behalf of your child.

DO keep a record of early intervention and school system officials you contact. Date your notes and highlight the salient parts of your conversation.

DON'T throw away the letters or the envelope when you receive correspondence from officials. The postmark on the envelope will help prove, for example, if a deadline was missed and serves to create a paper trail if you end up in a dispute over your child's special education services. Staple the envelope to the back of correspondence you receive.

DO take your own notes at any meeting held on behalf of your child and share the note taking with a spouse or family member who can take over when you have to stop writing to answer questions. Officials are likely to use their own note taker, but you can't always rely on the quality of their notes. Nevertheless, request a copy of all their notes.

DO ask questions and state your disagreements about services or placement. The notes will become part of the record in a legal proceeding.

DON'T be confrontational when you disagree with officials. If your emotions rise, stop for a moment and take a deep breath before responding.

DON'T go to an intervention plan meeting alone. Take your spouse or another family member. These meetings can be intimidating, especially if you don't know the procedures. Sometimes the intimidation is obvious; other times it is subtle.

DO dress appropriately. These are business meetings. Look the part.

DON'T allow officials to evaluate your child unless you give them permission in writing, after being provided with a clear written explanation of what testing is being proposed, why it is being proposed, and how it will be carried out. The law, however, allows observation by officials without parental consent.

If the school wishes to formally observe your child, it is often helpful to attend these observations and take your own notes. You do not have an automatic right to accompany school observers. But if the school wants to observe your child in a private setting or at home, you can insist on being present.

DO keep track of procedural timelines. Timelines begin as soon as you sign consent to have your child evaluated. There are also new procedures and timelines for due-process hearings. Some due-process hearings hinge on school system officials making procedural mistakes and missing deadlines for assessing and evaluating children and implementing special education services.

DON'T object to a school program unless you've seen it. You'll lose credibility. If you've filed for due process, now is the time to hire an expert, such as an educational advocate, to observe the program. Testimony from an expert is weighed more heavily than your opinion, even if you are well educated. Nonetheless, you still must observe the program.

DON'T consent to your child being made eligible for special education unless you agree with that decision. Once your child is in special education, you may disagree with the school's decisions but must request a due-process hearing if you wish to overturn the school district's plan. Be aware that once your child is in special education, the school does not need your signature in order to implement a change in placement. If the school recommends a change in placement, you must request a due-process hearing within ten days of the decision or the school is allowed to implement the change. Many parents assume that withholding their signature has legal significance after their child is in special ed. This is untrue and frequently leads parents to assume they have blocked a plan by refusing to sign it when what they really need to do is request a hearing.

DO monitor your child's progress once an intervention plan is implemented. Some parents require school therapists to keep a logbook of when they treated their child. Make sure you review it for completeness.

Testimony Prep: Preparing Yourself for the Witness Stand

Whether you seek to resolve a complaint against your school district in mediation or due process, you'll want to act with confidence when you're asked questions. Following these testimony guidelines, adapted and reprinted with permission from Margaret Kohn, Esq., should help you feel less nervous. Your attorney or educational advocate may offer additional advice.

▹ Listen carefully to each question.

▹ Request that a question be clarified before you answer. Ask to have the question rephrased, or state that you don't understand the question. Just say, "Can you ask the question another way?"

▶ Pause if there is an objection from anyone and wait until you are told whether to answer.

▶ If you forget the question, ask to have the question repeated.

▶ Take your time, and don't rush!

▶ Don't worry about speaking smoothly, hesitating, or saying "um." These things do not count against you.

▶ Say less rather than more.

▶ "I don't know" and "I don't remember" are perfectly okay answers.

▶ You and your lawyer are present to try and educate the hearing officer. Try to speak to him or her.

▶ If the hearing officer asks a question, try to answer it directly.

▶ Your lawyer is responsible for moving the proceeding along and handling anything unexpected. You just need to answer the questions.

▶ Don't preface your answers with (1) I'm not sure, but maybe it was . . . (2) Probably it was . . . (3) I'm not sure what happened back then but . . .

▶ Instead, try (1) It was in [give month], I'm not sure which day. (2) It was before [name holiday], but after [fill in blank]. (3) It happened before [name any big event or holiday in your life].

▶ Once you have begun your testimony, you are not allowed to consult with your attorney about your answers, but you can pass your attorney notes.

TEN

▶ ▶ ▶ **The Financial Toll:
Who Pays for What, and
How to Cope with the Strain
on Your Pocketbook**

While personal finance magazines encourage families to save for the future, when Leo was diagnosed, everyone around us said to spend now or we'd lose our opportunity. My attitude was that, for Leo, we'd find the money for whatever schools, therapies, or programs that might help him. If there was an opportunity for him to achieve independence through intensive early intervention, we were going to find the money because we had to.

We knew that spending $60,000 a year on Leo's therapy would murderously accelerate the rate at which David and I were depleting our savings. To be honest, I didn't want to think about the $1,000 a week I was spending on therapy or knowing how rapidly we were going into debt. Luckily, we had a small cushion of money to start with. While my parents had helped me out financially before, the amount necessary to have an impact on Leo's life was well beyond their resources. We used credit for living expenses, since I still wasn't earning a paycheck and considered getting a job impossible until Leo entered a full-day program, fully two years away.

While we had won twice at due process and gotten financial recompense, we never sought the total amount of what we had spent because my lawyer doubted we'd get reimbursed for everything, especially services not traditionally covered by public services. They included applied behavior analysis, auditory integration training, and Floortime.

Then, David lost his job and started a political action committee, which folded after the 2004 presidential election. After years of fiscal irresponsibility, we finally hit the wall. We could no longer pay the bigger mortgage, our bills, and the fees for Leo's occupational therapy. Facing the abyss, David was forced to ask friends for money, tapping ex-girlfriends, relatives, and Internet venture capitalists that we mutually knew from our days past.

When creditors called, I was unable to suppress the panic of losing our home. Where would we go? Some public housing project in Washington? A shelter? Would I be homeless? I could go home to my parents in Lorain, Ohio, but then what? What would happen to our family?

We discussed bankruptcy, but the thought repelled us, and frankly, we didn't really know what that meant at the time. We thought of losing our good credit rating, our credit cards, not to mention the embarrassment of it all, the shame. As much as I loved David, I was furious with him and with the world.

But in the same month Leo was admitted into Lowell, at a cost of $19,500 a year, David informed me that he'd met with a credit counselor. We had no choice but to file for bankruptcy, and we had to do it now because changes in federal bankruptcy law were due to take effect in October 2005, four months away. The new law would force us to reorganize our debts, but if we filed under the old law, we could wipe them out.

I told David that bankruptcy or no bankruptcy, Leo had to go to Lowell. We had to keep our house. With the two largest household expenditures inviolate, reductions would have to come from somewhere else, but I didn't care where. We retained a bankruptcy attorney.

Keeping the bankruptcy from the children was paramount. If they felt insecure, they'd get scared. I plowed ahead, producing elaborate early birthday parties for Lucas and Leo and buying gifts using my credit card, which still worked on occasion. David was horrified that I refused to adjust to the new circumstances, but I fell back on the rationale that our children didn't have to suffer. Then, my bankruptcy attorney said to stop using the Visa, because it violated the "loading up" rule, which forbids piling up more debt prior to filing for bankruptcy. Everything I bought from then on was cash only.

I began looking for work and found a lead in the newspaper. As much as I was still furious with David, I just wanted him to fix it. We pulled together as a family, out of necessity. As our financial situation degraded, I sent in forms signing Lucas and Leo up for an expensive summer camp, because I had already paid a $1,400 nonrefundable deposit. I had always longed for Leo and Lucas to go to the same camp, but now more than ever I needed them in someone else's care while I looked for a job. David had just started a new job.

On July 28, 2005, we filed for Chapter 7 bankruptcy, which would allow us to liquidate our debts rather than pay them off. I found work and started four days later, enabling us to make Leo's first tuition payment at Lowell. After Labor Day, Leo, who'd turned six in June, started preschool at Lowell, and Lucas, eight, entered third grade at Janney. At the end of the year, a federal bankruptcy court discharged our case, allowing us to keep our house and car, and clearing us of our debt. Within six months, we began again on the proper course—remaking our lives the way I and everyone else devoted to Leo's "recovery" remade his.

Honestly, I don't know whether it was primarily the cost of Leo's treatments, evaluations, lawyers, aides, and special programs, or David's failed political venture, that finally pushed us over the edge into bankruptcy. The two were a potent mix. As with most things, the truth is messy. I believe our financial downfall was a little bit of both. If we had talked more along the way, I may have seen that David's spending was the result of the stress he was under from the need to provide for us. David exercised poor judgment, but so did I when I made financial commitments that I considered beyond discussion or when I bought frivolous things as a coping mechanism to get me through the day, and I needed to get through one day to face the next.

Looking back, the financial disaster that we brought upon ourselves was the outgrowth, in at least some measure, of the medical crisis that had begun four years earlier. I feel, then as now, that blaming anyone—David or Leo or even myself—isn't productive. I need to learn to forgive since it is the start of beginning anew. Leo needs help growing up, and we still do, too, intelligently improvising just as I had from the moment Leo was diagnosed.

◄ PRACTICAL ADVICE ►

As a general rule, you can reach into four sacks of money to pay for your child's intervention plan—federal and state coffers, health insurance, and private sources. Some of you will be able to pull out more than others because some states have better rules and regulations. But even when the rules are on your side—and you follow them—you still might not get the services your child needs. The one attribute that will contribute to your success is perseverance and not taking "no" for an answer.

Money Sack #1: Federal Assistance

The Individuals with Disabilities Education Act (IDEA) gives your child rights that did not exist before 1975. Under this law, the federal government will technically pay for your child's early intervention program and provide a free education when your child is ready to go to school. This generally means in a public school, sometimes with a one-on-one aide or other supports. Sometimes, school districts contract with private special education schools when there are limited public school options, but this is not a given.

States implement IDEA with funding from the federal government, but the government never provides enough money to fund programs, leaving states under tremendous pressure to make up the difference or offer parents as few services as possible. The rules and regulations in each state vary as greatly as the peaks and plateaus of a mountain range. Some states charge fees for services, such as speech-language and occupational therapy, depending on your ability to pay. Some treatments, including applied behavior analysis, aren't covered or you'll have to fight for coverage.

If you're seeking early intervention services, it is not uncommon to be put on a waiting list to receive them, despite legal timelines that specify when critical services are to be delivered to infants and toddlers. For children transitioning out of early intervention services, about one-third who had an early intervention plan experienced a gap in services of nearly five months before they received preschool services by their school district, according to an August 2006 study by the National Center for Special Education Research. Because services are so bad in certain areas of the country, some families move to a state that offers more assistance for children with autism. Special education experts list Wisconsin, California, New York, and Maryland as examples of states that do the best job of implementing IDEA.

Before your child is awarded services under IDEA, he or she needs to meet eligibility requirements, which also differ from state to state. As of April 2007, almost 194,000 students ages six through twenty-one nationwide were identified with autism and receiving special education services under IDEA.

Many parents retain a special education attorney and/or an

educational advocate to navigate the maze. A special ed attorney should apprise you of state and federal law, while an educational advocate is likely to know more about how your school district operates. You may need both. Retaining either is expensive, and costs vary depending on where you live.

A U.S. Supreme Court ruling in May 2007 handed parents of disabled children a legal victory when it ruled that they could go to federal court without a lawyer to dispute their school district's plan for educating their child. If you choose that route, at least consider consulting with a lawyer to prepare yourself for court. See Chapters 8 and 9 for more about IDEA, how it works, and whom to call to get started.

SUPPLEMENTAL SECURITY INCOME

Another source of federal funds to help pay for your child's intervention plan includes the Supplemental Security Income (SSI) program, which is handled by the Social Security Administration and funded by U.S. Treasury funds. To apply, the paperwork is copious. The program pays benefits to disabled children from low-income families with minimal assets. The benefit is determined by where you live and your total earnings. Go to the Social Security Administration's homepage* and choose "Supplemental Security Income" from the "Frequently Asked Questions" pull-down menu. As a first step to see if you might qualify, use the Social Security Administration Benefit Eligibility Screening Tool,† which screens for SSI and Medicare. Social Security also publishes the free book *Benefits for Children with Disabilities.*‡

---

* www.ssa.gov
† http://best.ssa.gov
‡ www.socialsecurity.gov/pubs/10026.html

Money Sack #2: State Assistance

SPECIAL EDUCATION SCHOOL VOUCHERS

Increasingly, states are passing laws to help parents pay for their child's private education. This help comes by way of school vouchers. About thirteen states have them, but only four—Arizona, Florida, Georgia, and Utah—offer school vouchers, called scholarships, that target children with disabilities. Another state, Ohio, offers a scholarship for children diagnosed with autism. In fact, about 50 percent of the children served under the Ohio scholarship program are from three to five years old. As of September 2007, six states—Kentucky, Mississippi, Nevada, Oklahoma, South Carolina, and Texas—are considering special education vouchers.

The Autism Scholarship Program in Ohio, which applies to children as young as three years old, is the most generous, paying up to $17,000 a year per student. Most special education vouchers are much less, averaging between $4,800 in Utah and $6,927 in Florida. The amount you receive may still fall short of private school tuition. Eligibility criteria vary but generally require that your child be enrolled in a public school and have a current Individualized Education Program.

If you opt for a voucher, you'll have to waive your right to federal resources provided under IDEA. Beware: Vouchers can be revoked. In Florida, a child becomes ineligible if he or she returns to public school, and Ohio, which sends voucher payments directly to parents, will stop payment if the money isn't used to pay a private provider.

If you live in one of these states and want to find out more, locate the website of your state's department of education and use its search feature. All four programs with vouchers for autistic children are administered by your state's education agency. The formal names of the other programs are: McKay Scholarship Program

(Florida), Arizona Program for Pupils with Disabilities, and the Carson Smith Scholarship Program (Utah). Project Forum is another good source of information about special education vouchers. Get its report, *Special Education Voucher: Four State Approaches*.* School Choice Info† follows this issue.

AUTISM WAIVERS

Five states—Colorado, Indiana, Maryland, Wisconsin, and soon Massachusetts—offer waivers specific to autism. These waivers allow eligible children with an autism spectrum disorder to receive a range of services, such as applied behavior analysis (also known as intensive behavioral intervention) and psychological services, at no cost to the family. Families may also receive respite care and family support services. These waivers fall under Medicaid services, and waiver programs typically have long waiting lists or are closed to new applicants because all available slots are filled.

As of April 2006, forty-four other states and the District of Columbia offered developmental disability waiver programs, according to a 2006 General Accounting Office report on federal autism activities. Of the states that offer these waivers, five states— Alabama, Connecticut, Massachusetts, Mississippi, and Virginia— exclude autism in their definition of developmental disability, which means a child with autism won't be eligible unless the child also has mental retardation. Some states limit enrollment to those needing long-term institutional care, which means that children with higher functioning autism or Asperger's disorder wouldn't qualify. In some instances, the waiting list to receive a waiver to cover the cost of intensive behavioral intervention is so long that

* www.projectforum.org/docs/specialeducationvouchers-fourstateapproaches.pdf
† www.schoolchoiceinfo.org

children become ineligible once a slot opens up because the waiver sets an age limit for coverage.

To find a waiver program in your area, head over to the U.S. government's Centers for Medicare and Medicaid Services* and click on a state for details.

Money Sack #3: Health Insurance

Reform of state insurance laws to cover autism treatments is the area of greatest action. In June 2007, Texas became the eighteenth state to require insurers to cover autism treatments for very young children. A December 2006 report from the Connecticut Office of Legislative Research[†] summarizes how other states' insurance laws cover autism treatments.

The mandates range from "mental health parity" to coverage of specific treatments, such as applied behavior analysis. "Mental health parity" means equal insurance coverage for mental and physical illness. For example, if an insurer covers speech-language services for a stroke, a medical condition, then the insurer can't deny coverage of speech-language services for a child with autism, which is classified as a mental illness, despite its being listed as a neurobiological disorder in the official diagnostic handbook of psychological disorders. The Autism Bulletin blog[‡] posts updates on state legislative action (go to "Labels" and click on "health insurance").

The main reasons why insurers deny coverage of autism treatments is because they claim they are experimental and not their responsibility. They pin the responsibility on school systems to correct developmental disorders. Insurers also view autism as incurable and therefore not worthy of treatment. Despite all the reform,

---

* www.cms.hhs.gov/MedicaidStWaivProgDemoPGI/08_WavMap.asp
[†] www.cga.ct.gov/2006/rpt/2006-R-0793.htm
[‡] http://autismbulletin.blogspot.com

ask your child's health care provider to steer clear of the autism diagnosis codes 299.00, which is for autistic disorder, and 299.80, for Asperger's disorder. I was told that the diagnostic code 3444 might help get a special ed program paid for. Code 3444 stands for static encephalopathy, which means permanent or unchanging brain damage that is neither progressing nor regressing. The diagnostic code often accepted by insurance companies for occupational therapy is 781.3, a muscular disorder known as hypotonia. For psychological services, the oft-used diagnosis is 312.9—or disruptive behavior disorder, cause unknown—can be employed as a substitute code for autism. If in doubt, ask your doctor what codes insurers are covering.

Even if your child is insured through your health plan, reimbursement differs from plan to plan. It's a job to keep up with claims, and you may have to call multiple times to get a claim paid. Keeping a call log with the date and name of the person you contacted helps everyone, especially if claims stretch back several months. Every time you call, you're likely to talk to a different person, and that in itself is frustrating. If one insurance representative is giving you a tough time, hang up and call back. You'll get a new person who may be more responsive.

United Healthcare, which sells insurance, also offers grants of up to $5,000, with a lifetime limit of $7,500, to cover medical expenses not fully covered by a family's health insurance plan. Speech-language therapy and physical therapy are two examples of the types of services covered through its Children's Foundation.* The program targets individuals with little or no income and who are covered by a commercial health insurance plan. Families receiving Medicare, Medicaid, or any state or federally subsidized health insurance are not eligible, and grants cannot be used to pay for past medical expenses.

* www.uhccf.org

Federal and state governments also subsidize insurance programs for uninsured children. Visit Insure Kids Now* to find out about coverage and eligibility requirements in your state.

Money Sack #4: Private

A growing number of nonprofits across the country offer direct financial assistance in the form of grants to parents. They offer grants that are $1,500 or less, with the average grant about $500. Surely, any amount is helpful for a family in need, but this amount doesn't begin to solve the problem of paying for an intensive treatment program that ranges in cost from $60,000 to $100,000 a year.

Some nonprofits, such as the Helping Hands program run by the National Autism Society,† cover a broader range of treatments—including vitamins or nutritional supplements, such as cod liver oil and folic acid—than other nonprofits. ACT Today!‡ is another grant-issuing nonprofit. Most of the nonprofits offering these grants restrict applicants to a specific geographic location, and there may be a lengthy wait of six weeks or more to receive funds because of the often cumbersome application process. Their websites are often obscure. You can find others by entering the key phrase "direct financial assistance" together with the word "autism" in search engines.

CLINICAL TRIALS

Having your child participate in clinical trials, which are designed to evaluate new treatments, is a way to receive no-cost treatment. The National Institutes of Health (NIH) recruits participants

* www.insurekidsnow.gov
† www.nationalautismassociation.org/helpinghand.php
‡ www.act-today.org/grants.html

through ClinicalTrials.gov.* Participation in a clinical trial will allow your child to gain access to new treatments before they become widely available and contribute to medical research. If your child qualifies for a clinical trial, you won't know whether he or she will be randomly assigned to an intervention or drug under investigation. You also might check the websites of universities for clinical trials. Some offer free evaluations for certain studies. Although you won't have to pay for the cost of treatment, you will probably have to make and pay for your own travel arrangements. Thankfully, some non-profits offer programs to cut transportation and lodging costs. NIH maintains a page on its website that lists several resources.[†]

Tax Benefits

There are also tax benefits associated with raising a child with special needs. If your workplace offers a medical flexible spending plan, take advantage of it. This benefit allows a family to set aside up to $10,000 of earnings before taxes. Use this tax-free income to help pay for your child's special education school, and medical and psychological services. For a list of eligible expenses allowed by the IRS under this plan, get Publication 502, *Medical and Dental Expenses Including the Health Coverage Tax Credit.*[‡]

Creating a Paper Trail

As you navigate through a labyrinth of services and assistance, keep these other two points in mind: (1) Be tenacious about researching the reimbursement options in your state, and (2) take notes. Documenting

* www.clinicaltrial.gov
† http://rarediseases.info.nih.gov/asp/resources/pat_travel.asp
‡ www.irs.gov/pub/irs-pdf/p502.pdf

your experience will bolster your case in the event you seek legal recourse or mediation, or file an insurance appeal.

The initial organization and then maintenance of your child's file is one of the most difficult tasks for many parents, yet one of the most important. If you keep a neat, well-organized file, in chronological order, you will be able to find something quickly and gain a sense of self-control over a situation that is not likely to end soon.

You should also buy an electronic phone book. You don't need anything fancy or expensive, just something to store contact information. You will be filling out many forms, and having a handy place that stores your child's Social Security number, pediatrician's

▶ **INFORM YOURSELF**

The Arc of the United States has prepared Family Resource Guides for twenty-five states. The guides are not specific to autism benefits but are more general, covering mental retardation and related developmental disabilities. They are also several years out of date. Nonetheless, use them as a springboard to conduct your own research. The guides describe federal and state programs and their eligibility requirements and benefits. Visit the state-specific websites listed in the guides for current information on the programs listed. Visit The Arc* and choose "Resources" and then "Family Guides" to download them.

Insurance Help for Autism† is a site created by a mother who battled her health insurer in California to cover her child's autism treatments. While her step-by-step guide is targeted for families living in California, you should be able to adapt some of her advice to your specific situation. She also offers a sample insurance letter for obtaining coverage, which you'll need to customize for your state since it references laws and court cases in the state of California.

*www.thearc.org
† www.insurancehelpforautism.com/guide.html

contact information, as well as that of other experts your child sees will save time and lessen the aggravation.

Coping with the Costs

Under almost any circumstances, the diagnosis and care of a child with a medical condition is a financial challenge for a family. One or both parents quickly use up their vacation time, then lose time from work, and perhaps one parent quits work to manage his or her child's health full-time. There are at least two ways that autism and related disorders are financially more burdensome—urgency and the multiplicity of treatment techniques that you are responsible for evaluating and, in some cases, implementing at home.

I wish I could clue you in on "seven secrets" for coping with the financial strain, but it isn't so simple as earning more or spending less. What I can share is some insight on why certain families cope better than others, and the answer may surprise you.

The reason has more to do with your attitude about debt than your economic status. Certainly, if you have a robust bank account, you'll be able to absorb the financial aftershocks of paying for treatments that neither your insurance nor a publicly funded program covers.

You stand the best chance of surviving this as a financial disaster if you put your situation in an analytical framework rather than let irrational behaviors dominate. If you are half of a couple, chances are that one of you is the more methodical person. One of you needs to set out a financial plan, if possible, and both of you should strive to readjust your attitude about what you value most. Becoming less materialistic and feeling content with less are two important attributes for financial survival. Interestingly, these same attributes are what keep most people out of debt in the first place.

My financial coping strategies, I admit, were terrible. I practiced what psychologists call "escapist behavior." I hoped that divine intervention (in my case, David) would solve our problem. He didn't, try as he might. I also declined to change my spending patterns, which was another way I coped with the chaos of being under so much stress.

Upstairs in Leo's bedroom, the Spiderman head lamp glows red like a lollipop held up to light. Above the headboard, a picture of a rainbow embraces a child; a mother stands near; the sun smiles overhead. My eyes trace the rainbow's arc that forms a halo of red, yellow, green, and blue over his self-portrait, and then drop to the real boy splayed across the bed sleeping.

I breathe in time with him, kissing his cheek and running my hand across his arm. He's no longer a baby but a spirited eight-year-old boy. He's my little Leo. His curly flaxen hair, having darkened to the color of sand, is cut short. A band of freckles covers the bridge of his nose. At four feet tall, he has long, lean arms and legs, and his teeth are still set wide apart in his mouth. And his eyes, oh, his beautiful eyes; they have kept the arresting pool-blue color that makes me want to hug him.

Sometimes, I look at him and think about the eleven children Dr. Leo Kanner observed in his 1943 pivotal paper that differentiated autism from childhood schizophrenia and gave it the name

Leo and me, drawn in spring 2005.

"autism." Before early intervention, Leo's behavior was strikingly similar to the children Dr. Kanner observed. He paced in circles, confused his pronouns, made unintelligible sounds, engaged in valueless conversation, ignored people as if they were pieces of furniture, and didn't care about Santa Claus in his merry red suit.

If the children observed by Dr. Kanner are still alive, they are in their seventies. Donald T., I know from reading newspaper accounts, is seventy-three years old and apparently doing well in Forest, Mississippi. The era of his childhood, when Roosevelt led the nation to war with Germany and Frank Sinatra led the hit parade, seems long distant. But Donald T.'s mother had feelings identical to mine sixty years later. Dr. Kanner quotes her saying, "The thing that upsets me most is that I can't reach my baby."

Once I could not reach my baby and thought those very words, but that time has passed.

We still struggle with lingering residual issues. Leo reacts to frustration and challenges in immature ways; he is overly sensitive and cries too much, but now he has the self-awareness to realize this. When he has an outburst, he tells me, "A little alarm goes off in my head." He also has a controlling style of play. He likes to tell his peers what to do, and I can imagine him as a movie director someday. While his reading comprehension is good, he has anxiety about learning how to read and especially about playing team sports. He tells me, "Sports and I do not connect." He likes being around his peers, but he's not as physically adept.

Leo still struggles with controlling his emotions. We have turned to medication to help mitigate his sometimes-explosive personality. But medicating a child with poor self-regulation is difficult. We have had to experiment with medications, such as Prozac and Tenex, which were formulated for other purposes, in the hope of finding one that worked. While meds have helped Leo reduce anxiety and tolerate more frustration, he can still boil over and lash out when he cannot bend the world to his will. I'm confident he'll learn new and better ways to cope. But I do not yet know if drugs are a lifelong need or not.

But sometimes, his actions are governed by pure impulsive unconstrained desire. In Freudian terms, Leo is all Id. But he's only eight years old and not dissimilar to other children his age in this regard. He's still just a kid.

Sometimes I say things to Leo that I shouldn't. We were at Universal Studios in Orlando in August 2006, and Leo complained about the heat. I told Leo to shut up. I mistakenly thought that if I told him this, he'd realize that his complaining wears thin on me. But immediately I felt horrible and wished that I could take it back. Leo crouched to his knees and began to cry.

"I don't want to be your little miracle anymore," he said, rubbing his eyes, filled with tears. I knelt beside him and rubbed his back.

"I'm sorry, Leo," I said. "Mommy loves you. I didn't mean to say that. Please be my little miracle."

A Picture of Me

by Leo
drawn on the
first day of Pre-K

Self-portrait drawn in
September 2004.

Another self-portrait, a year and a half later.

I can upset myself if I dwell on Leo's next set of challenges, such as the pressures of being a teenager, so I do not ponder them. When I feel down, I remind myself of his remarkable progress. His report card from kindergarten is confirmation of what he has accomplished. On the last report, his teacher wrote:

Leo seems to grow and change daily. When he comes to school, he delights in entering the room to greet his peers and definitely gets the attention he is seeking. Having received this social affirmation, Leo is ready to begin his day, side-by-side, with other children. . . . Leo has incredi-

bly strong verbal language skills; his rich, descriptive vocabulary makes him a masterful storyteller.

If there was a breakthrough moment in our confidence in his future, it was returning from our vacation in Naples, Florida, to visit my parents when Leo was almost three. We were dropping off the rental car. The guy driving the shuttle van to return us to the airport had a slight accent so David asked him where he was from. He said Quebec, and they started conversing in French. Lucas and Leo occasionally hear their dad speak French, which he learned while living in Paris for a few years. We had one French children's book, a few French tapes, and every now and then David still begins translating their bedtime stories into French before the children shout him down with a demand to "speak English!"

David paused in his conversation with the driver and asked Lucas, then about five, if he knew any words in French. Lucas hummed and hawed, but Leo blurted out *"Voilà!"* After a moment of stunned silence, we all convulsed with laughter, first that Leo had riffled through his memory, located a word, and said it. But also because it was exactly the right word. Leo beamed. Later, David told me that he still felt a twinge of embarrassment at having not even addressed his question to Leo. I thought to myself that even if the word had come from memory more than reason, or even if it were a lucky guess, if Leo could do that, he was going to be all right.

"Voilà!" is emblematic of Leo's zest for life and what I like most about my son. He has a flamboyant personality and definite tastes in clothes that include wearing ties to preschool. We have these marvelous chats about, well, anything, and I secretly record many of our conversations that are too precious to be left to my sleep-deprived memory. On the eve of his seventh birthday, I caught this one about relationships and transcribed it.

LEO: Then comes the hard part.

ME: What's the hard part?

LEO: Getting your home.

ME: Yeah, that is a hard part. Most people don't have enough money to buy a home right away.

LEO: I mean, I don't.

ME: Well, it took Mommy and Daddy a long time.

LEO: And then comes the part where you have to buy a car.

ME: Right.

LEO: Aye, aye, aye. And do you know who has to do all that stuff?

ME: Who?

LEO: The dad.

ME: You think so?

LEO: That's what's going to be hard. I mean I have to buy the car. I have to build the house.

ME: Why wouldn't it be . . .

LEO: I practically have to ask the girl out.

ME: It's a lot of work, isn't it?

LEO: Yep. And the wife doesn't have to do anything except make the baby, for crying out loud.

ME: Well, that's a lot of work, too.

LEO: It's so hard.

Now that Leo no longer meets the diagnostic criteria that placed him on the autism spectrum, is he, as the clinicians like to put it, "indistinguishable from his peers"?

I believe that he is.

He continues to attend Lowell and is socially engaged, articulate, creative, and performing at grade level. He is no longer the little boy who once pitched his forehead into the sand, scooping up wet fistfuls to dribble on either side of his temples. He is a little boy who greets me with a panda bear mask he made in summer camp as he jumps into the backseat. And most importantly he has friends he cares about and who care about him.

Without a doubt, I believe Leo overcame his diagnosis because we intervened early. The treatments crucial to his recovery were the ones with the most scientifically proven strengths—applied verbal behavior and Floortime. He has achieved significant gains in areas thought to be unattainable by even high-functioning children with autistic spectrum disorders. Leo can form relationships. He can communicate. He can think. He can empathize. He has achieved the six milestones of Floortime.

The idea that a child can recover from an autism spectrum disorder is controversial. Skeptics will always argue that recovery is impossible because it is a lifelong brain disorder. Or if it was "cured," then it wasn't autism to begin with.

No one can say for sure how many children have recovered from autism. There are no nationwide recovery rates that are accepted by the medical establishment. Some data suggests the possibility of recovery and validates it over time,[13] but even this research is hotly debated. Moreover, there is no definition for recovery or even criteria to base it on.

Some children might never be able to converse, but success for them will come in other ways. It may be a first word, idea, or look in the eye, or a program that integrates them more successfully into school or with peers. It might be fleeting moments of engagement followed by the return to a self-referential world.

I don't know how to counsel parents to come to terms with a child who makes slow progress because that was not the path I was on. Some of my friends have gone so far as to have another child in order to change the dynamic in their household and help the challenged child. As much as I would like a third, I will turn fifty-four this fall. At my age, the risk of having a child with any kind of disability is too great, and I do not want to go through what I did with Leo again.

I don't understand mothers who say the experience of raising a child with special needs has enriched their lives so much that they wouldn't have it any other way. Leo has enriched my life, too, and given it purpose beyond material things. But that doesn't mean I'm happy it happened. I would have rather found other ways to gain sensitivity to people with disabilities. I would have gladly volunteered, donated money, anything but what our family went through. But it was my responsibility to rise to the challenge presented me.

After years of chaos, I have learned many lessons. I learned there was no one to hand this off to and that Leo was my responsibility to integrate into society. I learned to follow my instincts. I learned that I needed to be an advocate for my son when I was still learning what I was advocating for. When I became more fully aware of Leo's rights under the law, I made sure he got them. I learned to be more sensitive to other people with disabilities, though I have not entirely resolved my feelings about the disabled. It is hard to erase feelings that were instilled so many years ago when I was subtly taught to avoid people with imperfections. I also learned to educate myself so that I could make informed decisions about treatment options and school programs.

I learned to set aside time for myself and take a break when I got too overwhelmed by the voluminous amount of information I had to constantly process.

I'm not sure of the impact this experience will have on Lucas. On some level, he understands that his brother has challenges, and we will tell him more as time goes on. Lucas's reservoirs of goodwill are often breached and burst forth in frustration. But Lucas is also Leo's most skilled caregiver, able to calm him and bring him back to their play better than anyone. Because I have a tendency to overprotect Leo, I am perhaps closer to him. When my family of four "couples up," Lucas drifts to David and Leo runs to me. We are, as one of Leo's psychologists once said, "JayLeo." How true. Joined in life, yet separate in our lives. When Lucas does come to me, I'm there, to scratch his back and whisper "I love you" to him. I hope that as an adult Lucas will step up and help, if need be. As for now, Lucas prefers not to talk about the issues concerning Leo, though I keep trying to explore his feelings about this.

I have also learned to heal, but I am not healed. I feel that I have a silent fellowship with thousands of other parents who are healing with me and learning to accept their children for the unique individuals they are, no matter what the outcome.

As I look ahead, I imagine Leo as proud, happy, healthy, and successful. I also believe he will find true love. I take comfort in the words of his child psychiatrist who said, "There is a peer for everybody."

AUTISM OVERLOAD: WHERE TO FIND RELIABLE ONLINE INFORMATION ABOUT AUTISM

Oh, What a Tangled Web. . . .

—SIR WALTER SCOTT

In less than a decade, the Internet has become the tool du jour for the way we communicate and research information about autism spectrum disorders.

But the ease with which anybody can build a website, or start a blog, has made it increasingly difficult and frustrating to find reliable information. Conflicting advice, out-date-information, and just plain misinformation abounds.

This section cuts through the clutter and identifies online resources to steer you on the right path from the start. You don't need millions of websites on autism; you need only a few.

While I repeat some of these online resources in the "Inform Yourself" sections of the main book, most of them are new.

Since website links change and new resources appear daily, I'll also show you the newest ways to keep up with the latest information on autism.

For easy access to these resources, visit my website, which I update regularly, at www.jaynelytel.com/resources.html and download a special free file that you can then import into your Internet browser.

Keeping Up with Autism News

The old way to stay current with news about autism treatments, legislation, research, and legal rulings was to bookmark your favorite websites and blogs, and visit them for updates or sign up for their newsletters. That method is time-consuming and out-dated.

The new way to get fresh information about autism is to have the news come to you through an RSS feed, which is viewed through a single webpage.

To get started, you'll need to sign up for a reader (it's free) and then set up a connection between the reader and your favorite websites that offer RSS (Really Simple Syndication) feeds.

Follow these two steps:

STEP ONE

The single webpage that you will view your news through is called a "reader." You can get one from Google (http://reader.google.com). Other popular readers include Bloglines (www.bloglines.com) and Newsgator (www.newsgator.com).

Choose a reader and sign up for an account.

STEP TWO

For the reader to work, you need to find sites that provide news "feeds" and then subscribe to them through your reader. You can identify sites that do this by looking for the letters RSS or XML, or a fan of white radio waves, on small orange icons. Another indicator is if you see a rectangular icon with a plus sign and some text after it, such as Netvibes or My AOL.

To subscribe to the feed, click on one of these icons. One of two things will happen:

The webpage will display code. Ignore this and copy the Internet address and paste it into your reader. You'll need to open your reader and look for a link that says "add feed" or "add subscription" before you paste the Internet address you've just copied.

With other sites, you won't have to copy the address and paste it into your reader. You'll only have to click on the icon and then click on "Subscribe to this feed" (usually in a yellow rectangle), and the link will be automatically added to your reader.

Once you've subscribed to feeds, updates will begin appearing in your reader when you open it. You can subscribe to as many feeds as you want. I use the Google reader.

Below I've identified some autism feeds I use to stay current.

Autism News Feeds
Add these feeds to your favorite reader and stay current on autism news and blogs. If you don't have one, try the Google reader at http://readers.google.com.

Autism News from Medical News Today
www.medicalnewstoday.com/rss/autism.xml

Autism News from Science Daily
www.sciencedaily.com/rss/mind_brain/autism.xml

New York Times Autism News Feed
http://topics.nytimes.com/top/news/health/diseasesconditionsand
healthtopics/autism/index.html?8qa&rss=1

Medstory Web Search on Autism
www.medstory.com/rss?q=autism&af=true&c=true&s=Web&i=

Medworm Query on Autism
www.medworm.com/rss/userss.php?qu=autism&title=
MedWorm+Query%3A+autism

Autism Alert Services

A simpler but less comprehensive way to stay abreast of autism news is to subscribe to an email-alert service. These services allow you to enter a keyword and associate it with your email address. Every time new information appears with that keyword, you'll receive email alerting you to the update, with a link to click on to read more.

Google Alerts
www.google.com/alerts
Enter autism as the search term, specify the frequency and input your email address. Automatically conducts a custom seach on the keyword and then delivers relevant results to your mailbox, based on the frequency you specify.

Web Resources

ADVOCACY AND SPECIAL EDUCATION

Family Voices's Tips on Becoming an Advocate
www.familyvoices.org/Information/YouAreAnAdvocate.pdf

LD OnLine (Learning Disabilities OnLine)
www.ldonline.org

NICHCY's Building the Legacy
www.nichcy.org/training/contents.asp#ThemeE
Strength: Free training modules on the 2004 revisions to the Individuals with Disabilities Education Act. Although aimed at trainers, parents will glean useful information. See Module 16, Children with Disabilities Enrolled by Their Parents in Private School.

TASH (Formerly The Association for the Severely
Handicapped)
www.tash.org/index.html

The Technical Assistance Alliance for Parent Centers
www.taalliance.org
*Strength: Offers special skills workshops for parents of children
with special needs in each state.*

U.S. Department of Education
http://idea.ed.gov
Explains the Individuals with Disabilities Education Act and its
2004 revisions.

ALTERNATIVE MEDICINE

The GFCF Diet
www.GFCFdiet.com
*Guides parents through the process of starting a gluten-free,
casein-free diet and lists contacts for registerd dieticians throughout the United States.*

NIH National Center for Complementary and
Alternative Medicine
http://nccam.nih.gov
*Explores alternative healing practices in the context of rigorous
scientific testing. Use keywords for specific practices, such a
"dietary supplements" or "chelation," rather than autism in
general.*

THE FOOD ALLERGY AND ANAPHYLAXIS NETWORK
www.foodallergy.org
Comprehensive information about food allergies, including how to read an ingredient label (under "Downloads"), and cooking and dining do's and don'ts (see "Featured Topics").

AUDIO AND TV SHOWS

AUTISM ONE RADIO
www.autismone.org/radio

STANLEY GREENSPAN, M.D., PODCAST
www.invisnet.com/webradio
Transcripts stored at www.floortime.org/ft.php?page=Radio%20 Transcripts.

DAN MARINO CHILDNETT.TV
www.childnett.tv/videos/new_releases

AUTISM BLOGS

ANGELA MOUZAKITIS'S APPLIED BEHAVIOR ANALYSIS
http://appliedbehavioranalysis.blogspot.com

AUTISM DIVA
http://autismdiva.blogspot.com

MICHAEL GOLDBERG'S AUTISM BULLETIN
http://autismbulletin.blogspot.com

THE JOY OF AUTISM
http://joyofautism.blogspot.com

AUTISM EVENTS

THE AUTISM CALENDAR
www.sarnet.org/events

AUTISM NONPROFITS

AMERICAN ACADEMY OF CHILD AND ADOLESCENT PSYCHIATRY
www.aacap.org

ASPERGER SYNDROME AND HIGH FUNCTIONING
AUTISM ASSOCIATION
www.ahany.org

AUTISM SOCIETY OF AMERICA
www.autism-society.org

AUTISM SPEAKS (MERGED WITH CURE AUTISM NOW (CAN) AND
THE NATIONAL ALLIANCE OF AUTISM RESEARCH
www.autismspeaks.org

FAMILIES FOR EARLY AUTISM TREATMENT
www.feat.org

ONLINE ASPERGER SYNDROME INFORMATION AND SUPPORT
(KNOWN AS O.A.S.I.S.)
www.udel.edu/bkirby/asperger

ORGANIZATION FOR AUTISM RESEARCH
www.researchautism.org

SOCIETY FOR NEUROSCIENTISTS
www.sfn.org

TALK ABOUT CURING AUTISM
www.tacanow.org

BEHAVIORISM

ASSOCIATION FOR BEHAVIOR ANALYSIS INTERNATIONAL
www.abainternational.org/Special_Interests/AutGuidelines.pdf
*Consumer Guidelines for Identifying, Selecting, and Evaluating
Behavior Analysts Working with Individuals with Autism Spectrum Disorders.*

BEHAVIOR ANALYST CERTIFICATION BOARD
www.bacb.com
*Strength: Offers a Certificant Registry that allows users to search
for BACB analysts by ZIP code, city, state, or last name. Also
check out its "Consumer Information" section to read about the
proposed autism specialty credential.*

CAMBRIDGE CENTER FOR BEHAVIORAL STUDIES
www.behavior.org/autism
Strength: Clearly written articles that explain the principles of behavior analysis. Its "ABA and Autism" section is particularly well done.

EARLY WARNING SIGNS

AUTISM VIDEO GLOSSARY
www.autismspeaks.org/video/glossary.php
*More than 100 video clips highlight early warning signs of autism
and compares them to videos of typical behavior.*

CENTERS FOR DISEASE CONTROL AND PREVENTION
ACT EARLY CAMPAIGN
www.cdc.gov/ncbddd/autism/actearly

FIRST SIGNS
www.firstsigns.org

ENVIRONMENTAL HEALTH

ENVIRONMENTAL HEALTH PERSPECTIVES
www.ehponline.org
Peer-reviewed monthly journal on how the environment impacts human health.
Strength: Offers free, online access to full-text articles. Search for "autism."

UNIVERSITY OF CALIFORNIA DAVIS CENTER FOR CHILDREN'S
ENVIRONMENTAL HEALTH
www.vetmed.ucdavis.edu/cceh
Examines how toxic chemicals may influence the development of autism in children.

GOVERNMENT AGENCIES AND RESEARCH EFFORTS

Use the search function to find articles, news, and information about autism spectrum disorders.

AUTISM AND DEVELOPMENTAL DISABILITIES
MONITORING NETWORK
www.cdc.gov/ncbddd/autism/addm.htm

INTERAGENCY AUTISM COORDINATING COMMITTEE
www.nimh.nih.gov/autismiacc/index.cfm

NATIONAL INSTITUTE OF CHILD HEALTH AND
HUMAN DEVELOPMENT
www.nichd.nih.gov

NATIONAL INSTITUTE ON DEAFNESS AND OTHER
COMMUNICATION DISORDERS
www.nidcd.nih.gov

NATIONAL INSTITUTE OF ENVIRONMENTAL HEALTH SCIENCES
www.niehs.nih.gov

NATIONAL INSTITUTES OF HEALTH AUTISM RESEARCH NETWORK
www.autismresearchnetwork.org/AN
Strength: A springboard to links of the major university and medical research centers that focus on the causes, diagnosis, early detection, prevention, and treatment of autism.

NATIONAL INSTITUTE OF MENTAL HEALTH
www.nimh.nih.gov

NATIONAL INSTITUTE FOR NEUROLOGICAL DISORDERS
AND STROKE
www.ninds.nih.gov

HEALTH INSURANCE

MAP OF STATE AUTISM INSURANCE LAWS
http://autismbulletin.blogspot.com/2007/07/map-of-state-autism
-insurance-laws.html

CMS-1500 FORM SOFTWARE
www.smartform.com/e/free_forms/free-forms_insurances.htm
Fill in insurance claim form information and print out completed form. Saves essential information, such as name, address, insurance numbers, and so on. Requires installation of the AnyForm software (after trial period one-time cost is $99).

IMMUNIZATIONS

CENTERS FOR DISEASE CONTROL AND PREVENTION'S
VACCINE SAFETY
www.cdc.gov/od/science/iso/about_iso.htm

INSTITUTE FOR VACCINE SAFETY (JOHN HOPKINS BLOOMBERG
SCHOOL OF PUBLIC HEALTH)
www.cdc.gov/od/science/iso/about_iso.htm
Strength: Choose MMR and search for "autism" for a list of reports that trace the measles, mumps, and rubella-autism controversy.

NATIONAL NETWORK FOR IMMUNIZATION INFORMATION
www.immunizationinfo.org
Strength: Excellent article that answers the most frequently asked questions about thimerosal and its use as a preservative in vaccines. Search for "thimerosal" to find it.

LEGISLATION

ASSOCIATION OF UNIVERSITY CENTERS ON DISABILITIES
www.aucd.org
Strength: Provides summaries, fact sheets, and press releases on federal legislation related to autism (www.aucd.org/template/page .cfm?id=311).

AUTISM LEGISLATION PROJECT
www.autismlegislation.org/about.html
Strength: Plans to publish legal research about autism legislation (one to watch).

PHARMACEUTICAL INFORMATION

PDRHEALTH
www.pdrhealth.com/index.html
Look up "pharmaceuticals."

PROMISING TREATMENTS

APPLIED BEHAVIOR ANALYSIS
www.lovaas.com

APPLIED VERBAL BEHAVIOR
www.behavioranalysts.com

FLOORTIME
www.icdl.com

TEACCH (TREATMENT AND EDUCATION OF AUTISTIC AND
RELATED COMMUNICATION-HANDICAPPED CHILDREN)
www.teacch.com

RESEARCH ARTICLES AND JOURNALS (ABSTRACTS FREE BUT GENERALLY NOT FULL-TEXT ARTICLES)

FOCUS ON AUTISM AND OTHER DEVELOPMENTAL DISABILITIES
www.proedinc.com/customer/productView.aspx?ID=1649

JOURNAL OF DEVELOPMENTAL PROCESSES (REPLACES THE
JOURNAL OF DEVELOPMENTAL AND LEARNING DISORDERS)
www.icdl.com/staging/bookstore/journal/index.shtml

HIGHBEAM RESEARCH
www.highbeam.com
*Access to full-text articles from medical and psychology journals
and major daily newspapers and magazines. Fee based.*

MEDLINE SEARCHES
www.bmj.com/cgi/content/full/315/7101/180
"How to Read a Paper: The Medline Database" introduces the nonexpert to searching the medical literature and evaluating the quality of medical articles.

NATIONAL CENTER FOR SPECIAL EDUCATION RESEARCH
http://ies.ed.gov/ncser/pubs
The U.S. Department of Education's primary research arm.
Strength: Read the April 2007 report "Secondary School Experiences of Students With Autism," under the Publications and Products page.

NATIONAL NETWORK FOR CHILD CARE
www.nncc.org
Rich collection of more more than 1,000 research-based and peer-reviewed publications and resources related to child care.
Strength: See "Articles and Resources" section and go to "Children with Special Needs."

THE COCHRANE COLLABORATION
www.cochrane.org
Read summaries of controlled trials in health care, including trials related to autism treatments. To read full-text articles, go to the Cochrane Library.

THE COCHRANE LIBRARY
www3.interscience.wiley.com/cgi-bin/mrwhome/106568753/
HOME
Collection of databases that offers high-quality, independent evidence on health-care topics. Cochrane has organized autism information by topic, but it takes some work to find it. Click "By

Topic," then choose "Developmental, Psychosocial, and Learning Problems." From the next list, choose "Developmental Problems," then "Autistic Spectrum Disorder."

SOCIAL AND EMOTIONAL GROWTH

EARLY SOCIAL INTERACTION PROJECT
http://esi.fsu.edu
Florida State University's Early Social Interaction Project aims to increase knowledge and understanding of effective, intensive early intervention strategies for very young children with autism spectrum disorders.
Strength: Visit the "Materials" section and get the free handouts on "Critical Information for Parents of Young Children with Social Communication Delays" and "The Importance of Early Intervention."

MICHIGAN ASSOCIATION OF INFANT MENTAL HEALTH
www.mi-aimh.msu.edu/intro/index.html
Strength: Order the Baby Stages and Preschool Stages wheels. Turn the dial to a child's age to find out what's going on with her social and emotional development and what parents and caregivers can do to nuture healthy development. The Baby Stages wheel goes from birth to thirty-six months. The preschool wheel starts at two years and ends at five years.

ZERO TO THREE: NATIONAL CENTER FOR INFANTS, TODDLERS, AND FAMILES
www.zerotothree.org
Comprehensive site on early childhood development (birth to three years old).
Strength: Key topics on brain development, and social and emotional development.

SPANISH RESOURCES

Asociación Nuevo Horizonte
www.autismo.com

El Autismo
www.nichcy.org/pubs/spanish/fs1stxt.htm
National Dissemination Center for Children with Disabilities's autism fact sheet.

SPECIALIZED WEB GUIDES

These websites have developed special sections on autism.

American Academy of Pediatrics
www.aap.org/healthtopics/autism.cfm

Autisminfo.com
www.autisminfo.com

Autism Wikis
www.wikia.com/wiki/wikia
Several wikis related to autism. Search for "autism" to find them. Note: A wiki is an online resource that allows users to edit and add content collectively.

Neurodiversity.com
www.neurodiversity.com/main.html
One of the most complete directories of autism information and resources.

New York Times — Times Topics
http://topics.nytimes.com/top/news/health/diseasesconditionsand
healthtopics/autism/index.html?8qa

TUFTS UNIVERSITY CHILD AND FAMILY WEB GUIDE
www.cfw.tufts.edu/topic/1/52.htm

YALE DEVELOPMENTAL DISABILITIES CLINIC
http://info.med.yale.edu/chldstdy/autism/links.html

Further Reading

Here is a discrete collection of the many autism books on book-shelves today. Visit my bookshelf on Shelfari at www.shelfari.com/jayne/shelf for updates.

National Research Council. *Educating Children with Autism.* Washington, DC: National Academy Press, 2001.

Sussman, Fern. *More Than Words.* Toronto: Hanen Centre, 1999.

Hodgdon, Linda A. *Visual Strategies for Improving Communication.* Troy, MI: Quirk Roberts Publishing, 1995.

Neisworth, John T., and Pamela S. Wolfe. *The Autism Encyclopedia.* Baltimore, MD: Brookes Publishing Company, 2004.

Greenspan, Stanley I., and Serena Wieder. *Engaging Autism.* Cambridge, MA: Da Capo Lifelong Books, 2006.

Greenspan, Stanley I., Serena Wieder, and Robin Simons. *The Child with Special Needs: Encouraging Emotional and Intellectual Growth.* New York: Perseus Books, 1998.

Schreibman, Laura. *The Science and Fiction of Autism.* Cambridge, MA: Harvard University Press, 2005.

Exkorn, Karen Siff. *The Autism Sourcebook: Everything You Need to Know About Diagnosis, Treatment, Coping, and Healing.* New York: HarperCollins, 2005.

Kranowitz, Carol Stock. *The Out-of-Sync Child: Recognizing and Coping with Sensory Processing Disorder, Revised Edition.* New York: Perigee Books, 2006.

Furth, Hans G., and Harry Wachs. *Thinking Goes to School: Piaget's Theory in Practice.* New York: Oxford University Press, 1975.

Weissbluth, Marc. *Healthy Sleep Habits, Healthy Child, 3rd edition.* New York: Ballantine Books, 2005.

McCall, Renee M., and Diane H. Craft. *Moving With a Purpose: Developing Programs for Preschoolers of All Abilities.* Champaign, IL: Human Kinetics Publishers, 2000.

Maurice, Catherine, Gina Green, and Stephen C. Luce. *Behavioral Intervention for Young Children With Autism: A Manual for Parents and Professionals.* Austin, TX: Pro-Ed Inc., 1996.

ENDNOTES

1. M. Sigman and E. Ruskin, "Continuity and Change in the Social Competence of Children with Autism, Down Syndrome, and Developmental Delays," *Monographs of the Society of Research in Child Development* 64 (1999): 1–114.

2. American Psychiatric Association, *Diagnostic and Statistical Manual of Mental Disorders: DSM-IV-TR*, 4th ed. (text revision), Washington, DC: American Psychiatric Association, 2000.

3. D. S. Mandell, M. M. Novak, and C. D. Zubritsky, "Factors Associated with Age of Diagnosis Among Children with Autism Spectrum Disorders," *Pediatrics* 116, no. 6 (2005): 1480.

4. D. S. Mandell, J. Listerud, S. E. Levy, and J. A. Pinto-Martin, "Race Differences in the Age of Diagnosis Among Medicaid-Eligible Children with Autism," *Journal of the American Academy of Child and Adolescent Psychiatry* 41, no. 12 (2002): 1447–53.

5. C. Lord, "Follow-up of Two-Year-Olds Referred for Possible Autism," *Journal of Child Psychology and Psychiatry* 36 (1995): 1365–82.

6. Behavior Analysts, Inc. Available at www.behavioranalysts.com. Accessed September 2007.

7. K. English, H. Goldstein, and K. Kaczmarek, "Promoting Interactions Among Preschoolers with and without Disabilities: Effects of a Buddy Skills-Training Program," *Exceptional Children* 63, no. 2 (1997): 229–43.

8. F. M. Gresham, M. E. Beebe-Frankenberger, and D. L. MacMillan, "A Selective Review of Treatments for Children with Autism: Description and Methodological Considerations," *School Psychology Review* 28 (1999): 559–76.

S. J. Rogers, "Empirically Supported Comprehensive Treatments for Young Children with Autism," *Journal of Clinical Child Psychology* 27 (1998): 168–79.

9. U.S. Department of Health and Human Services, "Mental Health: A Report of the Surgeon General," Rockville, MD: Department of Health and Human Services, 1999. Available at www.surgeongeneral.gov/library/mentalhealth/home.html. Accessed September 2007.

10. R. P. Goin-Kochel, et al., "Parental Reports on the Use of Treatments and Therapies for Children with Autism Spectrum Disorders," *Research in Autism Spectrum Disorders* 1, no. 3 (2007): 195–209. [i:10.1016/j.rasd.2006.08.006]

11. American Academy of Pediatrics, *Understanding Autism Spectrum Disorders (ASDs)*, Washington, DC: American Academy of Pediatrics, 2006.

12. U.S. Supreme Court, *Board of Education v. Amy Rowley*, 458 U. S. 176 (1982) at 200–01. Available at www.wrightslaw.com/law/caselaw/ussupct.rowley.htm. Accessed September 2007.

13. O. I. Lovaas, "Behavioral Treatment and Normal Educational and Intellectual Functioning in Young Autistic Children," *Journal of Consulting and Clinical Psychology* 55 (1987): 3–9.

    J. J. McEachin, T. Smith, and O. I. Lovaas, "Long-Term Outcome for Children with Autism Who Received Early Intensive Behavioral Treatment," *American Journal on Mental Retardation* 4 (1993): 359–72.

    R. Perry, I. Cohen, and R. DeCarlo, "Case Study: Deterioration, Autism, and Recovery in Two Siblings," *Journal of the American Academy of Child and Adolescent Psychiatry* 34 (1995): 232–37.

BIBLIOGRAPHY

American Psychiatric Association, *Diagnostic and Statistical Manual* (Washington, DC: APA Press, 1980).

P. Howlin, "Outcomes in Autism Spectrum Disorders," in *Handbook of Autism and Pervasive Developmental Disorders*, vol. 1, eds. F. R. Volkmar, A. Klin, R. Paul, and D. J. Cohen (Hoboken, NJ: Wiley, 2005): 201–22.

L. Kanner, "Autistic Disturbances of Affective Contact," *Nervous Child* 2 (1943): 217–50.

National Research Council, *Educating Young Children with Autism* (Washington, DC: National Academy Press, 2001).

F. R. Volkmar, C. Lord, et al., "Autism and Pervasive Developmental Disorders," *Journal of Child Psychology and Psychiatry and Allied Disciplines* 45, no. 1 (2004): 135–70.

INDEX

Page numbers in **bold** indicate tables; those in *italic* indicate photographs; those followed by "n" indicate footnotes.

236   Index

ABOUT THE AUTHOR

Photo by Andrea Boober

Jayne Lytel was born in Lorain, Ohio, and attended the University of Florida, where she majored in political science. She began her career as a journalist, covering federal policy affecting Wall Street and the bond market. In 1993, she launched the first publication devoted to the rise of the Internet as the commercial medium and spoke on behalf of the U.S. government on it. She capped her career as a nationally syndicated columnist for United Features Syndicate, Inc., before her son was diagnosed with autism. Her passion for helping families confront autism stems from her experience that early intervention is the best weapon against autism. After her son's recovery, Lytel founded The Early Intervention Network in 2007 and serves as its Executive Director. She also serves on the Executive Committee of the Autism Society of America's Northern Virginia chapter. Lytel lives in Washington, DC, with her husband, David, their two sons, and two cats.

Jayne's email address is jayne@actearly.org. For more information about the Early Intervention Network, visit www.actearly.org. Her personal website about the book is www.jaynelytel.com.